# UNDERGROUND

# UNDERGROUND

DAVID MACAULAY

HOUGHTON MIFFLIN COMPANY BOSTON

For ELIZABETH the saboteur

and JANICE the defender.

Also Available in Sandpiper Paperbound Editions

CATHEDRAL: *The Story of Its Construction*
CASTLE
PYRAMID

For time, information, encouragement, and sometimes all three, very special thanks in order of appearance to Larry Walsh, Bev Chaney, and Frank Dyckman in New York; John J. Doherty, Frank P. Bruno, Alan Gass, Clement Titcomb, Ben Kilgore, Tom Walsh, Tom Joyce, John Sullivan, James E. Wagner, George M. Pease, Frank J. McPartlan, Melanie and Walter in Boston; Lorraine Shemesh, Tom Sgouros, Bill Drew, and Wilbur Yoder in Providence; and Ruth Crossley-Holland somewhere on the Victoria line.

```
Library of Congress Cataloging in Publication Data

Macaulay, David.
   Underground.

   SUMMARY:  Text and drawings describe the subways,
sewers, building foundations, telephone and power sys-
tems, columns, cables, pipes, tunnels, and other under-
ground elements of a large modern city.
   1.  Underground utility lines--Juvenile literature.
2.  Underground construction--Juvenile literature.
[1.  Underground utility lines.  2.  Underground construc-
tion.  3.  City and town life]  I.  Title.
TD159.3.M3          624'.19          76-13868
ISBN 0-395-24739-X
```

Printed in the United States of America
RNF HOR
PAP CRW    20  19  18
ISBN 0-395-24739-X Reinforced Edition
ISBN 0-395-34065-9 Sandpiper Paperbound Edition

Beneath the buildings and streets of a modern city exists the network of walls, columns, cables, pipes, and tunnels required to satisfy the basic needs of its inhabitants. The larger the city, the more intricate this network becomes. While the walls and columns support the city's buildings, bridges, and towers, the cables, pipes, and tunnels carry life-sustaining elements such as water, electricity, and gas. Larger tunnels burrow through the underground, linking places on the congested surface more directly. Through them high-speed trains carry the large numbers of people who live and work within the urban community.

Since this massive root system is rarely seen, even in part, its complexity is difficult to imagine and its efficiency hardly ever realized. Not until the subway breaks down or a water main bursts do we begin to feel the extent of our dependence on this vast hidden network.

The primary purpose of this book is to expose a typical section of that network and to explain how it works. In order to limit myself to the more essential systems in the underground, I have invented a site at the intersection of two streets. Although the information is accurate, the step-by-step way in which it is presented is somewhat idealistic. In most cities, especially those that have grown gradually over many years, the various functions are all happening at the same time and often in the same place.

By better understanding the things we can't see in a familiar environment such as the city, we can learn to appreciate the array of unseen structures and systems, both manmade and natural, which surround us wherever we go. These amazing and often indispensable systems work so well and so quietly that we tend to be unaware of their existence.

COMING SOON
LUXURY OFFICE
SPACE
TEL 725-1355

POLICE

p. 52

p. 89

p. 86

p. 76

p. 79

p. 87

LORRAINE'S
ADULT BOOKS

WHAT TO LOOK FOR
ON THE STREET
AND WHERE TO FIND IT
IN THE BOOK

27

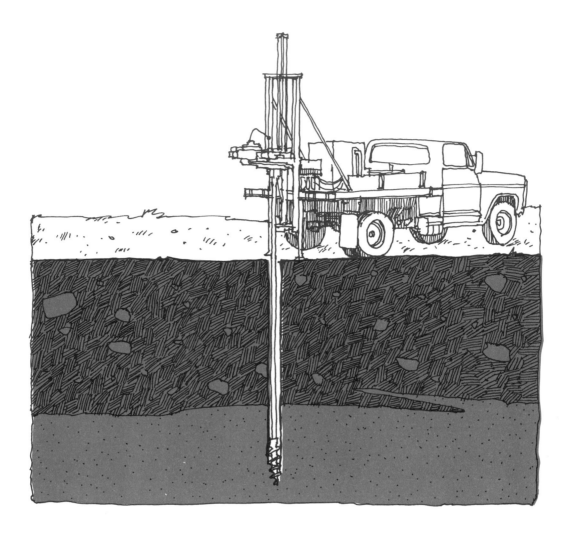

Most buildings are constructed on that part of the earth's surface that is composed of layers of material including sand, clay, miscellaneous rock, and water. Below them, often hundreds of feet, lies the solid crust of the earth called bedrock. Before a building can be completely designed, the architect must know the exact composition of the ground on which it will stand. This can be determined in several ways.

The simplest method is to dig a hole and look. But this only works if the hole doesn't have to be too deep. A second method uses an instrument called a sounding rod, which indicates the distance to bedrock. The best method involves using a variety of techniques for removing samples of soil and rock from various depths and examining them first hand.

No matter which method is used, all the tests are made at predetermined points marked on a plan of the site. The results are recorded on a vertical cross-section drawing that produces a picture of the site called a soil profile. It shows not only the kinds and depths of different layers but also the height of the water table. This is the distance below the surface at which the soil is completely saturated with water.

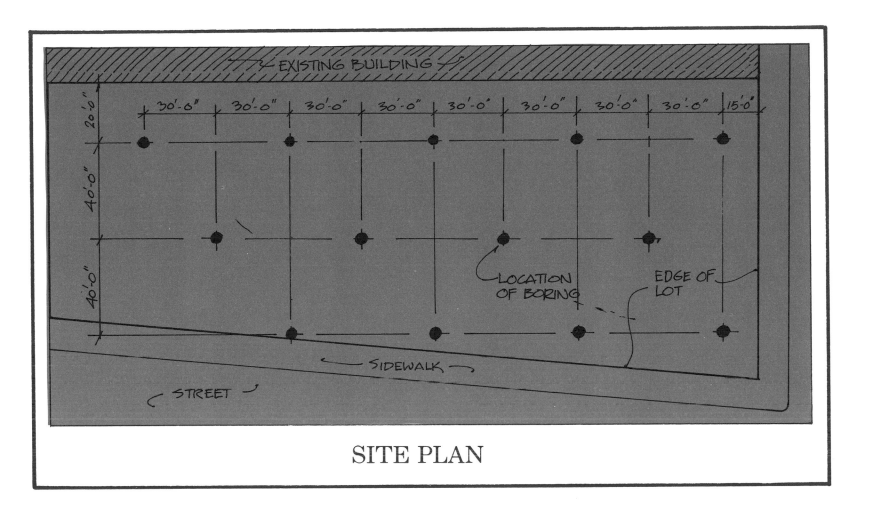

SITE PLAN

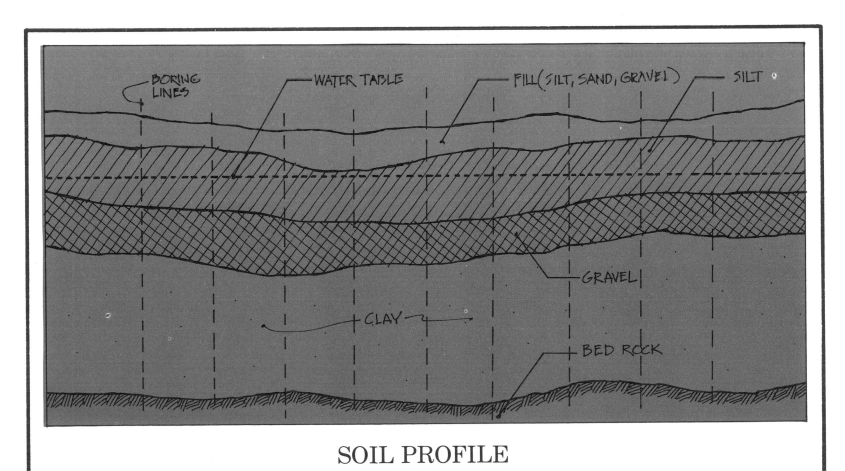

SOIL PROFILE

firm bearing soil or bedrock

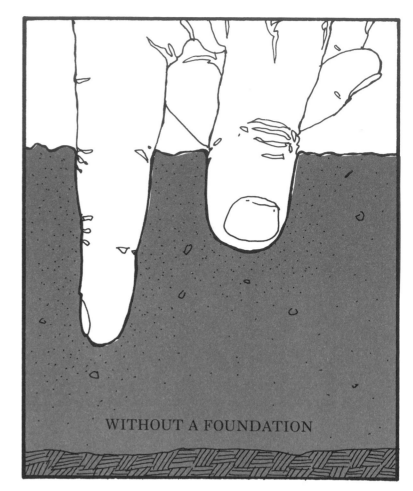

WITHOUT A FOUNDATION

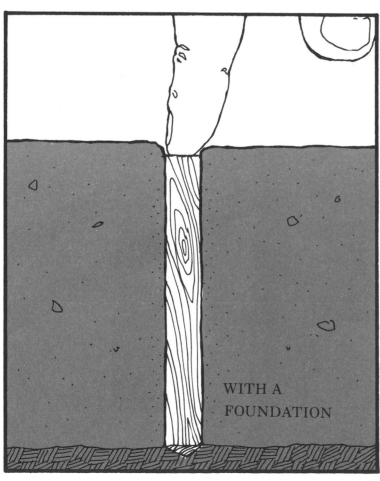

WITH A
FOUNDATION

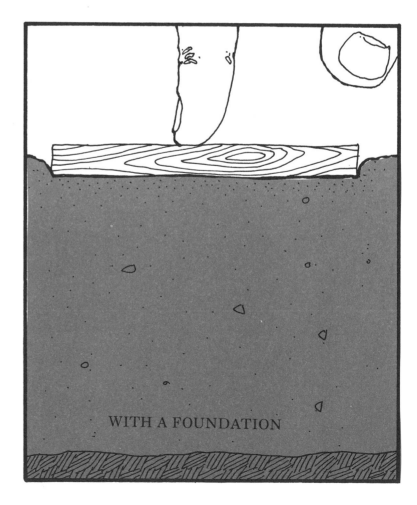

WITH A FOUNDATION

Bedrock is the best material on which to build. However, when bedrock is too far below the surface, foundations must be constructed that will either reach it or will enable the building to stand without reaching it. A foundation is the structure built to transfer the weight of a building to the material below. Since all buildings move or settle somewhat during and after construction, the foundation must also provide for uniform settlement. If one part of a structure moves more quickly or in a different direction than another part, serious weakening can occur. This aspect of foundation design is especially important when the ground below a building is unstable.

The best foundation for a particular building is determined by the weight of the building, the area over which that weight is to be distributed, and the soil conditions. The type of foundation used for most small buildings is called a spread foundation. It involves placing a flat concrete slab called a footing under each column or foundation wall. A footing simply spreads the weight placed on it over a greater area, thus increasing the resistance of the soil to the pressure.

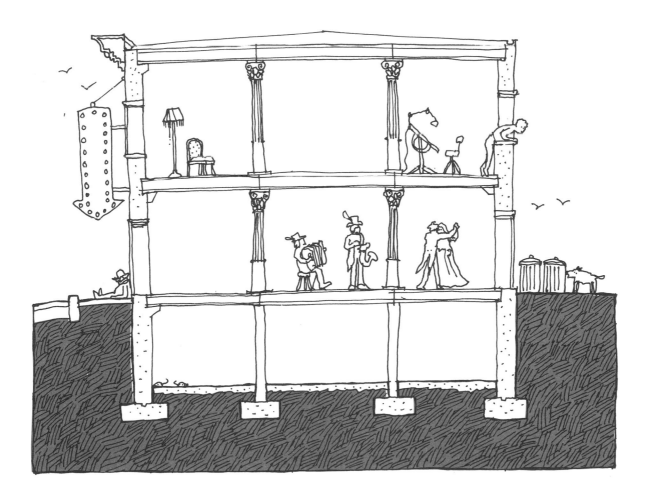

Concrete is a mixture of sand, lime, crushed stone, and water. It is trucked to the site as a liquid in rotating cylindrical tanks that keep the ingredients properly mixed. Concrete can be made into any shape by pouring it into the appropriate mold. The mold or form is removed as soon as the concrete hardens enough to stand by itself.

In order to construct a simple spread footing and foundation wall, a trench is first dug to the required depth. If necessary, it is then lined with vertical boards to prevent the soil from caving in. The boards, called lagging, are braced by heavy beams inserted between opposite walls. Once any water in the hole has been pumped out, preparations can be made for the concrete work. The form for the footing is a continuous shallow trough whose wooden sides are anchored into the ground and braced regularly across the top. A row of parallel steel rods, called reinforcing rods,

 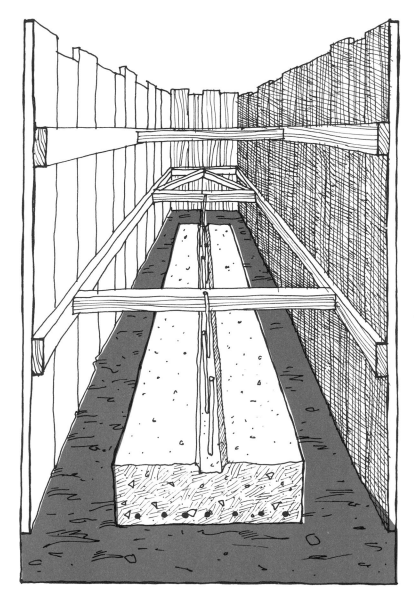

is placed inside the form a few inches off the ground. A second set, bent to rise above the form, will eventually be connected to the wall itself. A narrow groove is often formed down the center of the top of the footing to strengthen the connection between it and the foundation wall. Either steel rods or steel mesh are usually embedded in concrete to strengthen it. When they are in place, the form is filled.

The form for the foundation wall is made of plywood sheets and is set directly on top of the new footing. When one side has been erected, the reinforcing rods are installed. Then the second side is fastened to the first with steel ties and the entire form is braced to the lagging. It takes several weeks after the concrete has been poured for it to reach its maximum strength. For the first few days a certain temperature and amount of moisture must be maintained. It is for this reason that freshly poured concrete is often covered with straw or sheets of plastic.

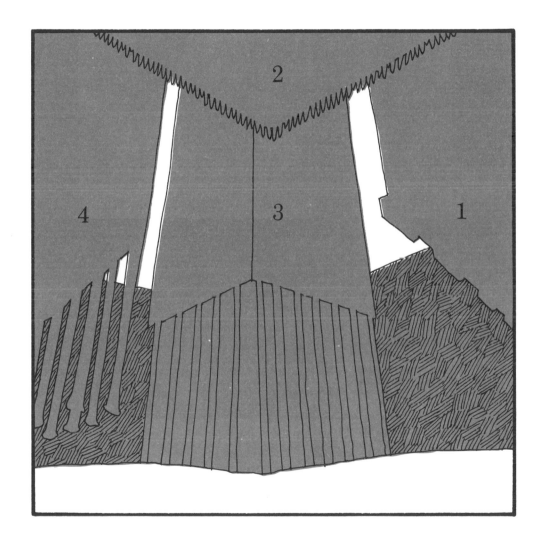

Foundations for larger buildings are generally adaptations or combinations of the four types used at our intersection. Building number one is on a floating foundation, number two on friction piles, number three on bearing piles, and number four on piers.

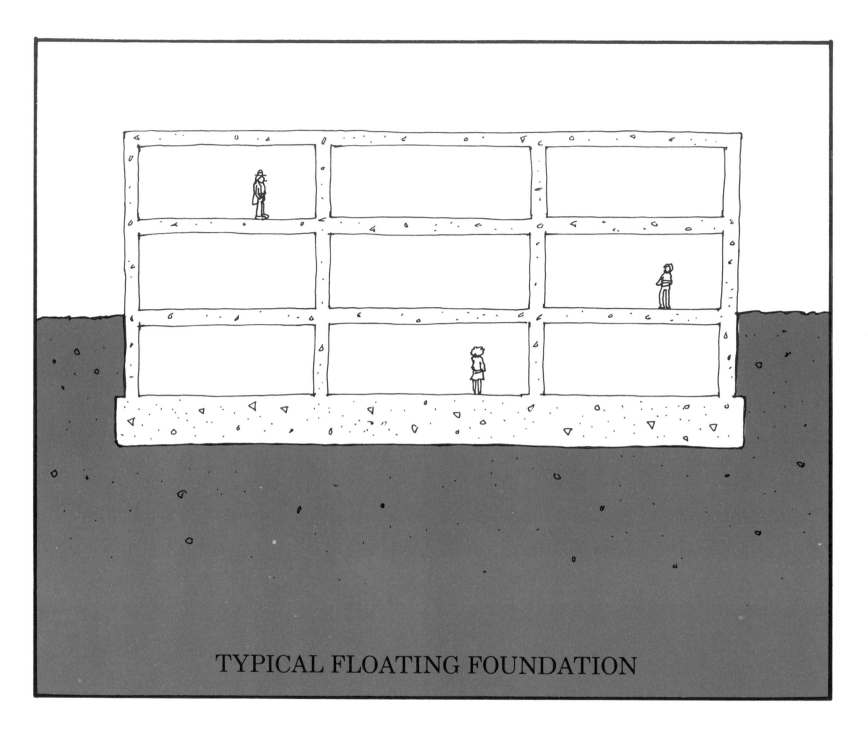

## TYPICAL FLOATING FOUNDATION

A floating foundation is basically a continuous spread foundation. Rather than placing many separate footings under a building, the entire structure is supported on a single reinforced concrete slab. It is used when the soil conditions are unstable and when the area of the site is great enough to carry the distributed load.

A second method of supporting a structure on unstable ground is to construct the building on friction piles. These are shafts hammered into the ground either vertically or at an angle, as required. Since a friction pile never reaches firm soil, its stability is created by the pressure or friction developed between the surface of the pile and the soil into which it is forced. Friction piles are grouped in rows or

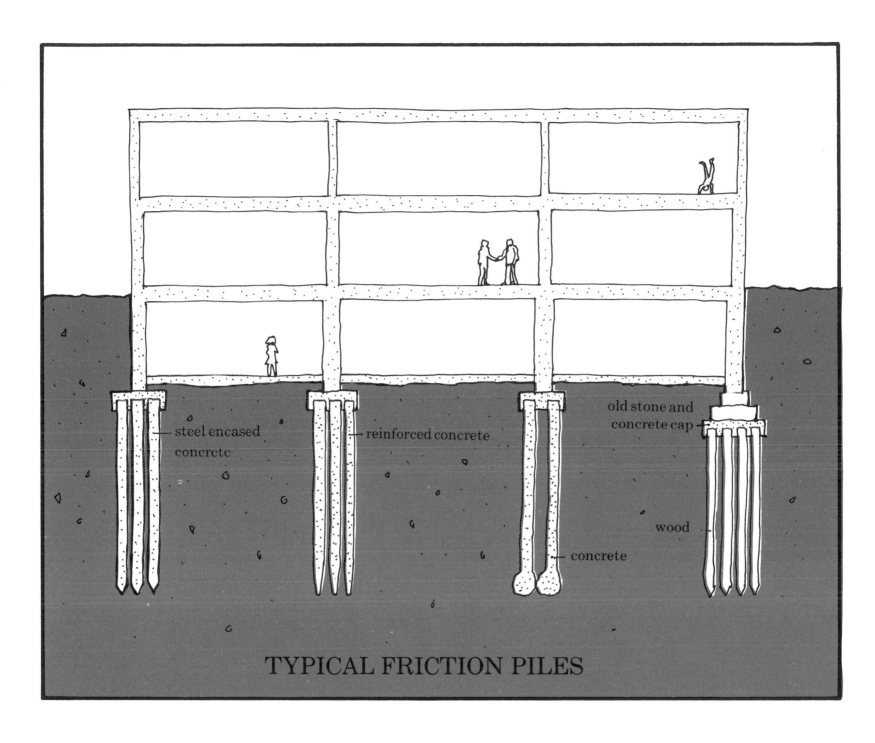

TYPICAL FRICTION PILES

steel encased concrete

reinforced concrete

concrete

old stone and concrete cap

wood

clusters depending on whether they support walls or columns. Once driven to the prescribed depth, their tops are connected by a concrete pad called a cap. The cap acts like a footing in that it distributes a portion of the load from above to each of the piles below. Today most friction piles are made of concrete and steel, but from ancient Rome into the twentieth century tree trunks stripped of their bark have been used. If a wooden pile is kept below the water table and therefore saturated, it can last indefinitely. If the water level drops, however, the exposed timber will dry out and rot.

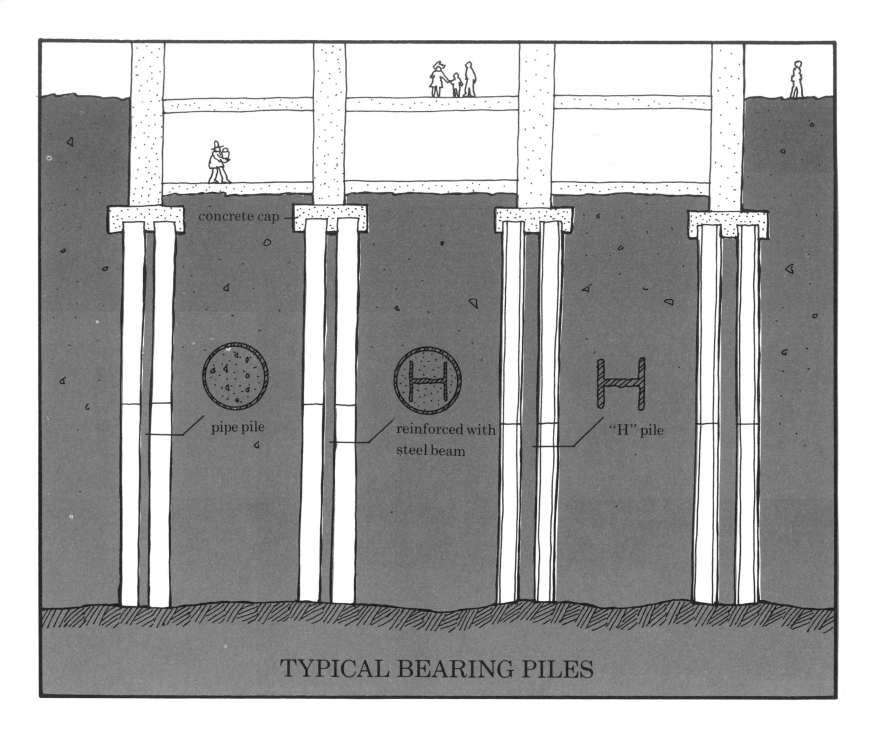

concrete cap

pipe pile

reinforced with
steel beam

"H" pile

## TYPICAL BEARING PILES

While a friction pile transmits the load along its length, a bearing pile is intended to transmit its load through the bottom to firm soil, such as clay, or bedrock. Bearing piles are therefore much longer, some reaching depths of over two hundred feet. Most are made of concrete and steel, although shorter ones can be made of wood. The two types most common in deep foundations are a hollow steel tube called a pipe pile, which once in place is filled with concrete, and a steel beam whose cross section resembles an "H," called an "H" pile. Both types are driven in sections and grouped into clusters capped by reinforced concrete slabs.

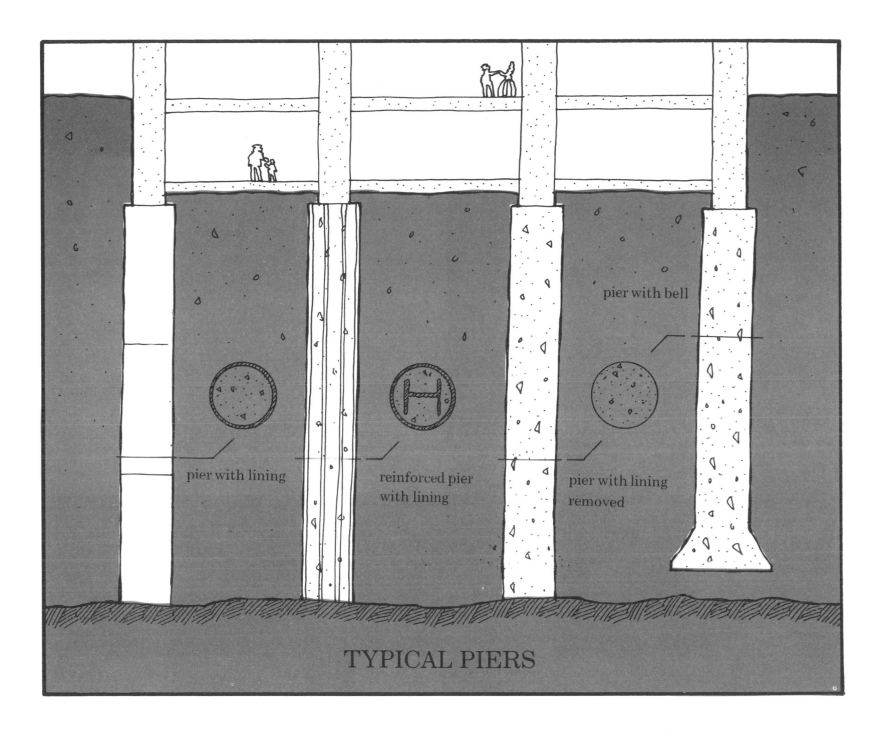

pier with bell

pier with lining

reinforced pier
with lining

pier with lining
removed

TYPICAL PIERS

Piers, like bearing piles, transmit most of their load through the base into firm bearing material. They can be any shape and are basically constructed by removing a column of earth and replacing it with concrete. If a pier does not rest on bedrock, its base is usually widened or "belled out" to increase the area over which the load is distributed. During excavation a lining of wood or steel is inserted into the hole to prevent the sides from collapsing. This lining can either be left in or pulled out as the concrete is being poured. A single pier is used in place of a pile cluster and therefore requires no cap.

Before construction begins, much of the soil at a site is removed. This process, called excavation, serves two purposes. First, it enables the foundation to be built on soil below the surface, which is usually more stable. And second, if piles or piers are to be used, it automatically reduces the distance they have to be driven or drilled.

Before excavation can begin, several precautions are taken to insure the stability of buildings in the area. The load on a foundation creates pressure in the surrounding soil, which might extend a considerable distance. For this reason any uncontrolled removal of soil can endanger existing structures many feet away.

If an excavation is to be deep and its sides vertical, the entire site must first be

enclosed by a retaining wall. Once the wall is properly braced it will resist the tendency of the soil to cave in, thus maintaining the necessary stability throughout the area. When the wall is built of steel or wood or a combination of the two, it is called sheeting. One type of sheeting consists of steel beams called soldier beams, which are driven into the ground at intervals around the site. Then as the soil is removed, horizontal boards are inserted between them. Another type consists of interlocking steel sheets called sheet piles which are driven into place before any soil is removed. In both cases, as the site is excavated, the sheeting is braced with inclined beams called shores, or by extending clusters of steel rods called anchors through the sheeting into the soil or rock outside the excavation.

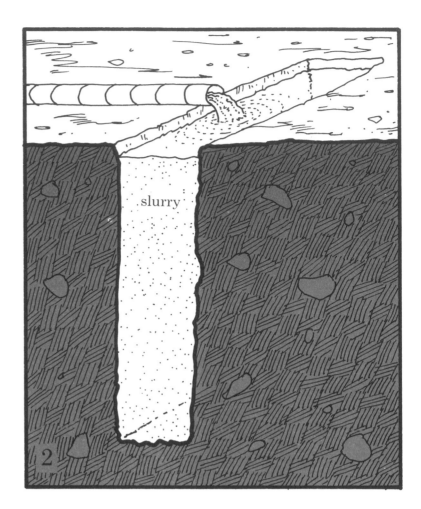

slurry

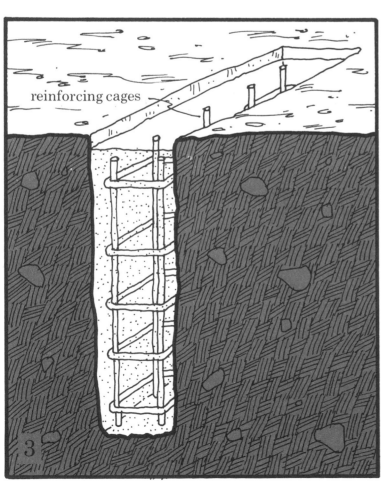

reinforcing cages

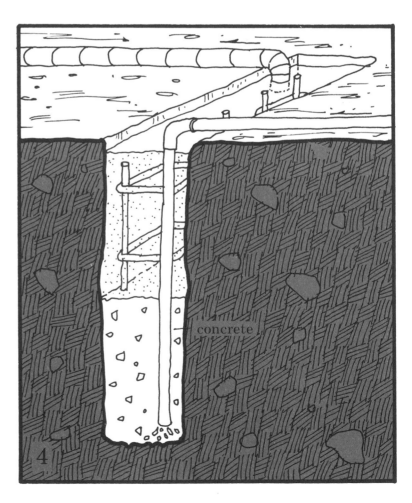

concrete

Another method of enclosing the site prior to excavation involves building a concrete wall either to bedrock or to a level below that of the new foundation. In order that the trench can be dug without lagging or bracing, which would be impractical at such a depth, as the soil is excavated, the hole is filled with a special mixture called slurry. This mixture is heavy enough to prevent the walls of the trench from collapsing, thereby preventing any change in the overall soil pressure. The trench is dug in lengths of twenty feet. When it reaches its final depth, pre-assembled cages of steel reinforcing are slid down through the slurry. The concrete is then forced into the trench through a steel tube. As the level of the concrete gradually rises, the slurry that is forced out of the top of the trench is pumped into storage tanks to be used again. Once it has set, the slurry wall is anchored into the surrounding soil or rock.

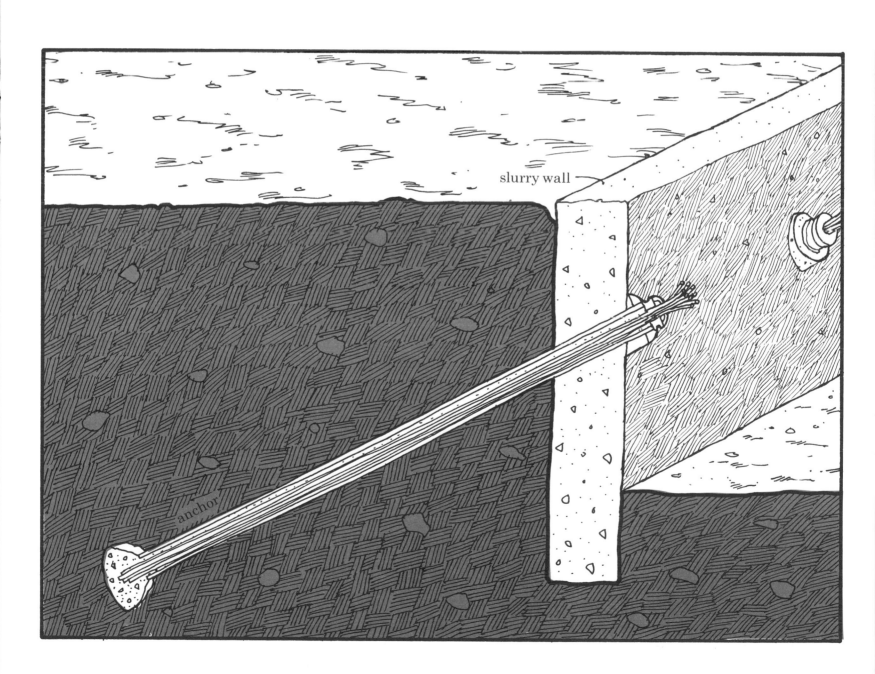

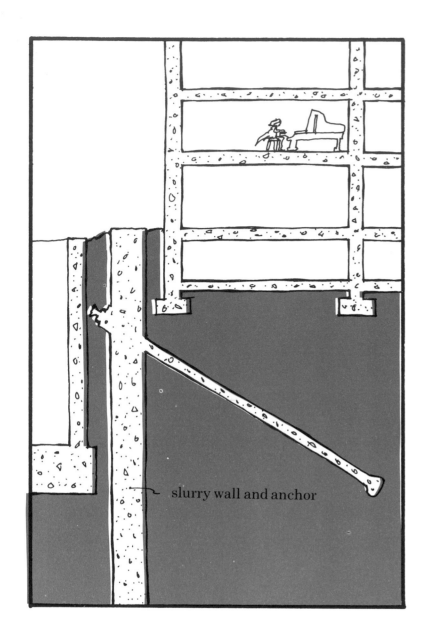

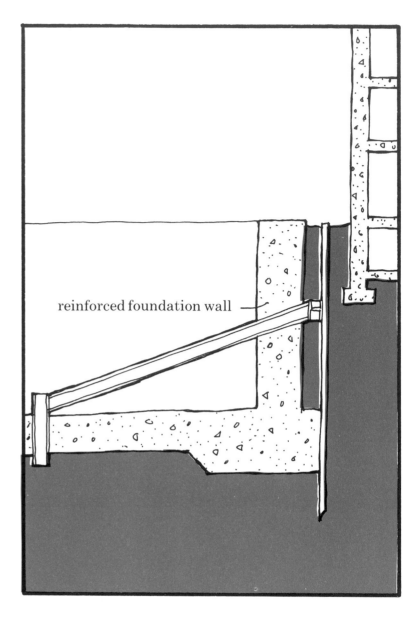

slurry wall and anchor

reinforced foundation wall

Both the slurry wall and the sheet piles are often used in areas with a high water table. Also used in these areas are a series of pipes called well points, which are driven into the ground to a point below the base of the excavation. They are connected to pumps that remove water when it is necessary to maintain a controlled water level. This process, however, must be carefully watched. If water is continually pumped from the soil in the excavation it will eventually lower the water table in the surrounding area. Any sizable reduction in the amount of ground water can increase the compactness of the soil, which in turn can affect the stability of existing foundations. For this reason it is sometimes necessary to pump water into the surrounding area through pipes similar to well points while at the same time removing it from the site. The last major problem that must be solved before work can begin occurs when the foundation of a building adjacent to the site is situated at a level

higher than the intended excavation. Once the hole is dug, there is a tendency for the existing foundation to slip sideways into it. This horizontal pressure can be resisted or eliminated in several ways. One method is to build and anchor a slurry wall adjacent to the existing building. Another method involves the use of sheet piling while a specially strengthened foundation wall is constructed for the new building that would take both horizontal and vertical pressure.

Other methods require that temporary support called underpinning be placed below the wall while the existing foundation is either extended or entirely replaced. The underpinning can consist either of horizontal steel beams called needle beams, which are placed through holes in the wall, or of pipe piles, which are driven in under the foundation. In either case the weight of the wall is removed from the soil immediately below it so it can be excavated and a new foundation constructed.

All these precautions must be taken before any work can begin on the foundations of the four buildings at our intersection. The soil at site number one is removed from one area at a time until reasonably firm ground is reached. If this necessitates digging beyond the required depth of the foundation, the floor of the excavation is rebuilt with compacted soil, gravel, or crushed stone. Once this is done the exact location of walls and columns is marked. Below the main columns, where the slab thickness increases, rectangular cavities with sloping walls are dug. The surface of

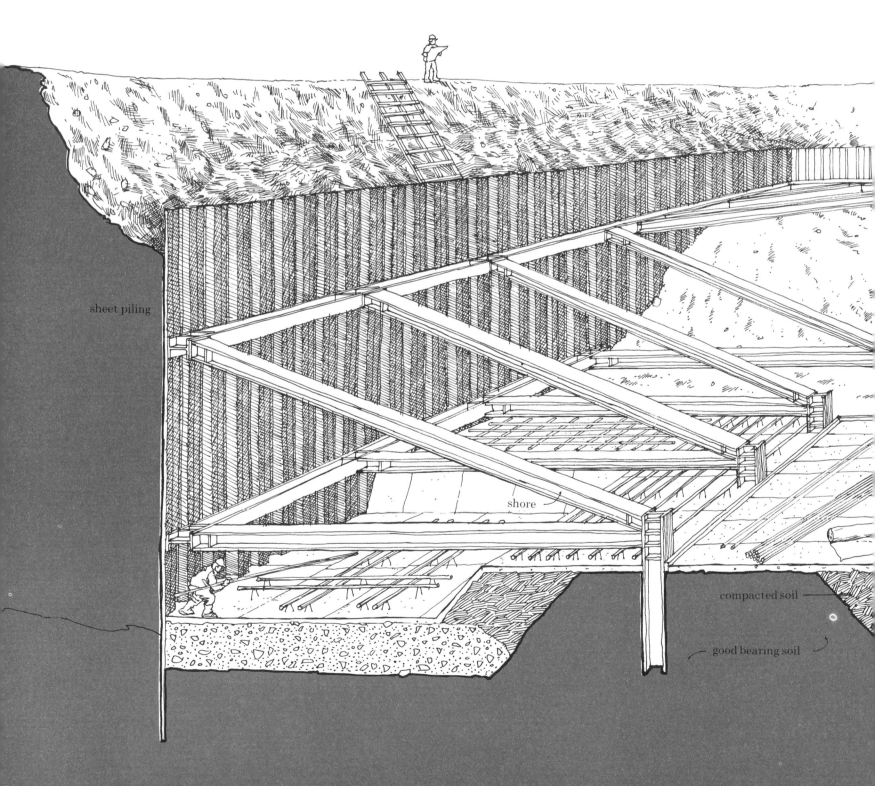

sheet piling

shore

compacted soil

good bearing soil

the excavation must be carefully prepared because it will serve as the form for the base of the spread foundation. In some cases the ground is lined with a three-inch layer of concrete called a mud mat to create a sturdier and more accurate form. Whether or not the mud mat is used, plastic waterproof sheeting is spread over the site before the finished slab is poured. Many layers of reinforcing rods are then carefully placed starting a few inches above the waterproofing.

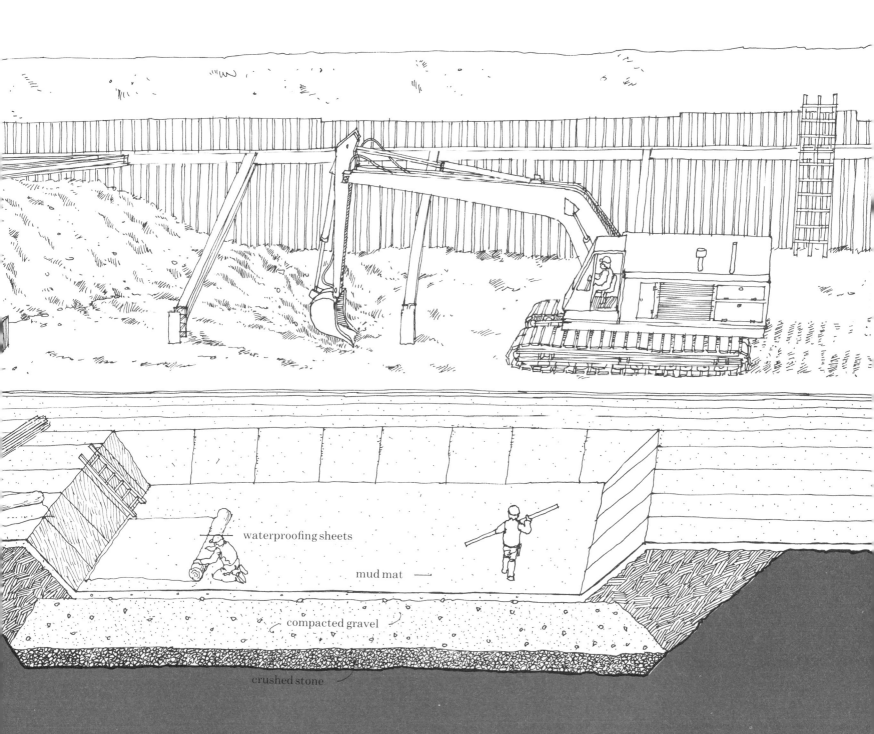

waterproofing sheets

mud mat

compacted gravel

crushed stone

Because of the size and thickness of this slab, it is poured in sections. When the reinforcing in a particular area is ready, a vertical form is constructed around it. The concrete is then pumped in through a flexible tube to insure that it fills all the spaces. As soon as the concrete reaches its desired strength, work starts on the columns and sections of wall it will support. A thick steel plate is set into the

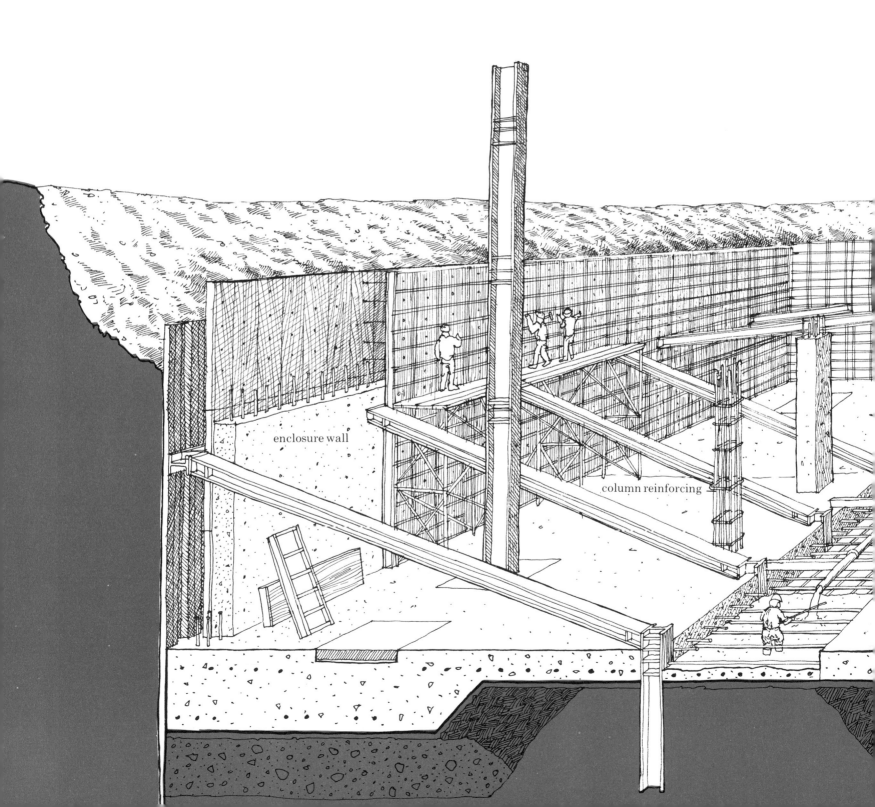

enclosure wall

column reinforcing

slab at each column location and carefully leveled. The plate is needed to prevent the steel column from crushing the concrete directly under it. As the columns are secured to the plates, a high concrete enclosure wall is constructed around the perimeter of the slab. Once it reaches maximum hardness, its exterior face is coated with a tarlike waterproofing material.

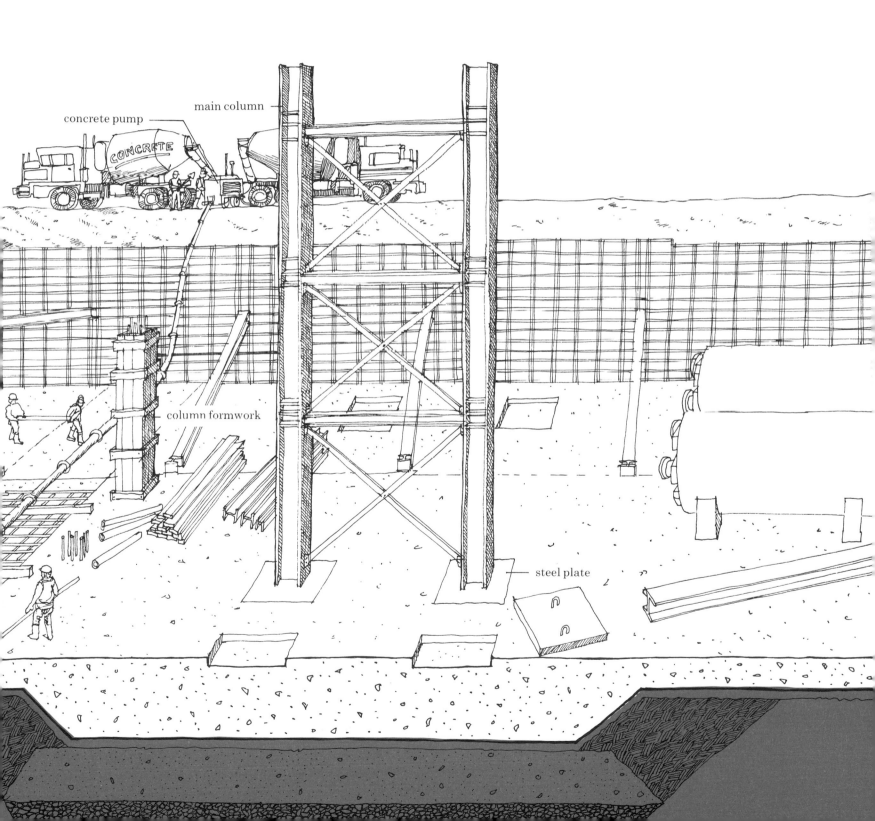

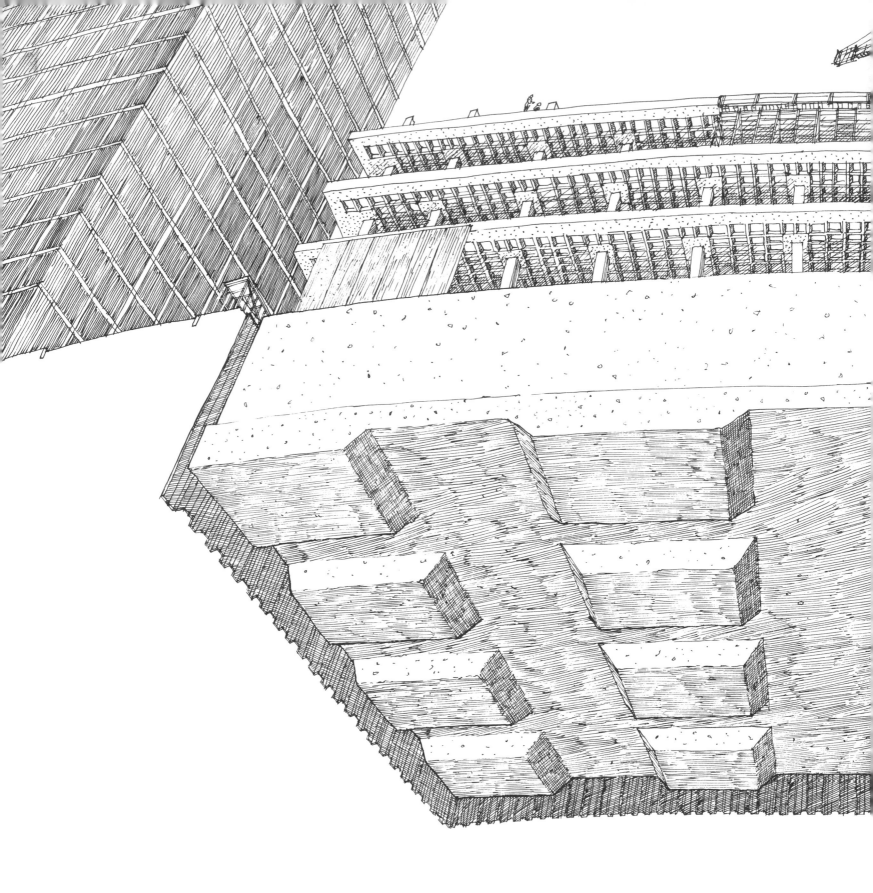

When this process is completed, the space between the wall and the sheeting is

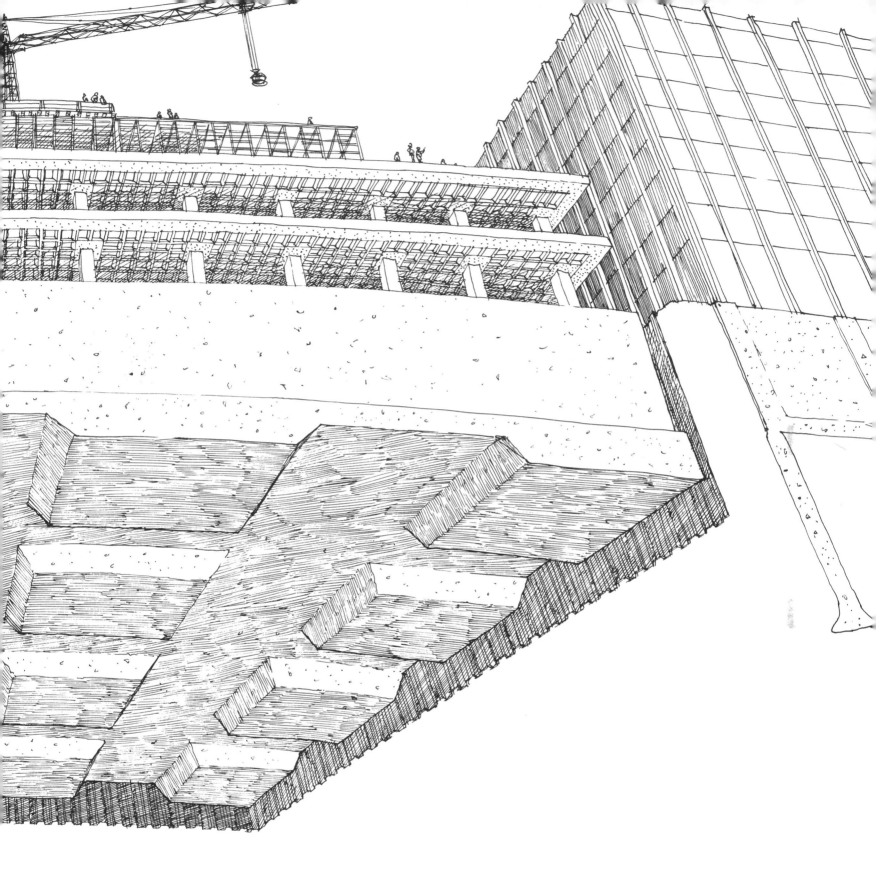

filled with packed soil and gravel. When all underground work is completed, the
sheet pilings are either removed or simply cut off below ground level.

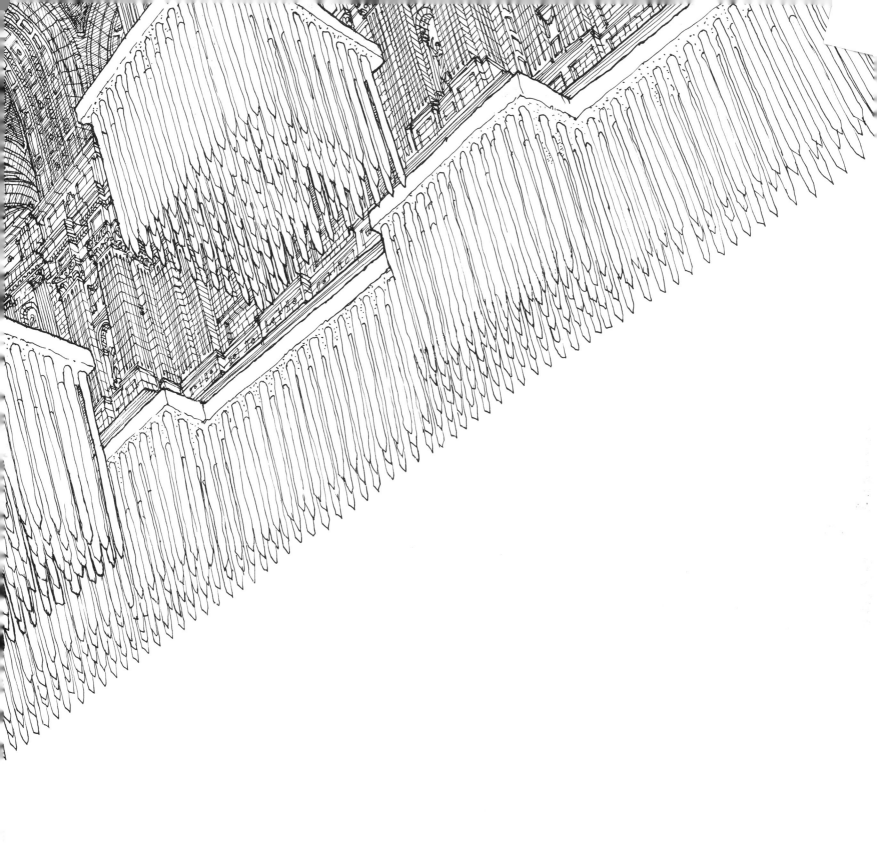

Building number two is the oldest building at the intersection and the only one
built of stone. Its walls and columns are supported on wooden friction piles.

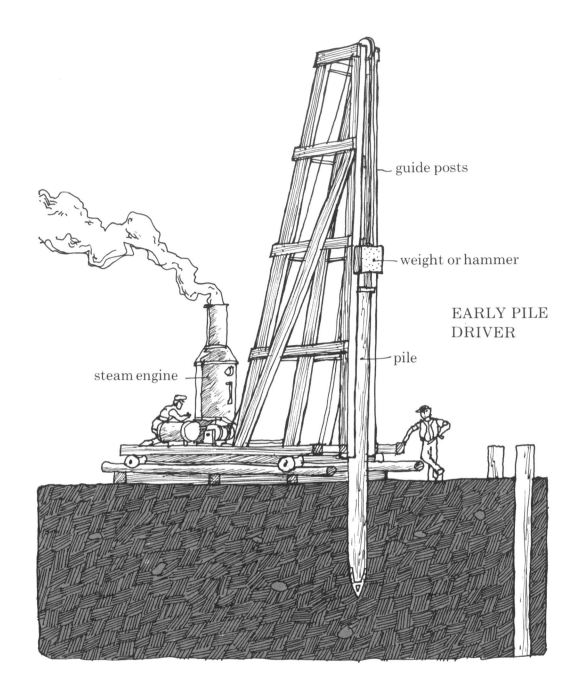

guide posts

weight or hammer

EARLY PILE
DRIVER

pile

steam engine

A pile is driven into the ground by the repeated blows of a weight supported above it between two guide posts. Several test piles are usually driven first at different locations across the site. By applying pressure to each and carefully measuring the rate of settlement, it is possible to determine the exact load that each pile in a particular area is able to carry. Because of the enormous concentration of weight, clusters consisting of hundreds of piles are required under each of the four main columns. The piles are driven into the ground about two feet apart to a point fifty feet below the surface. The main clusters are capped by wood-reinforced concrete and granite blocks. The outer walls rest on similar caps supported by parallel rows of piles.

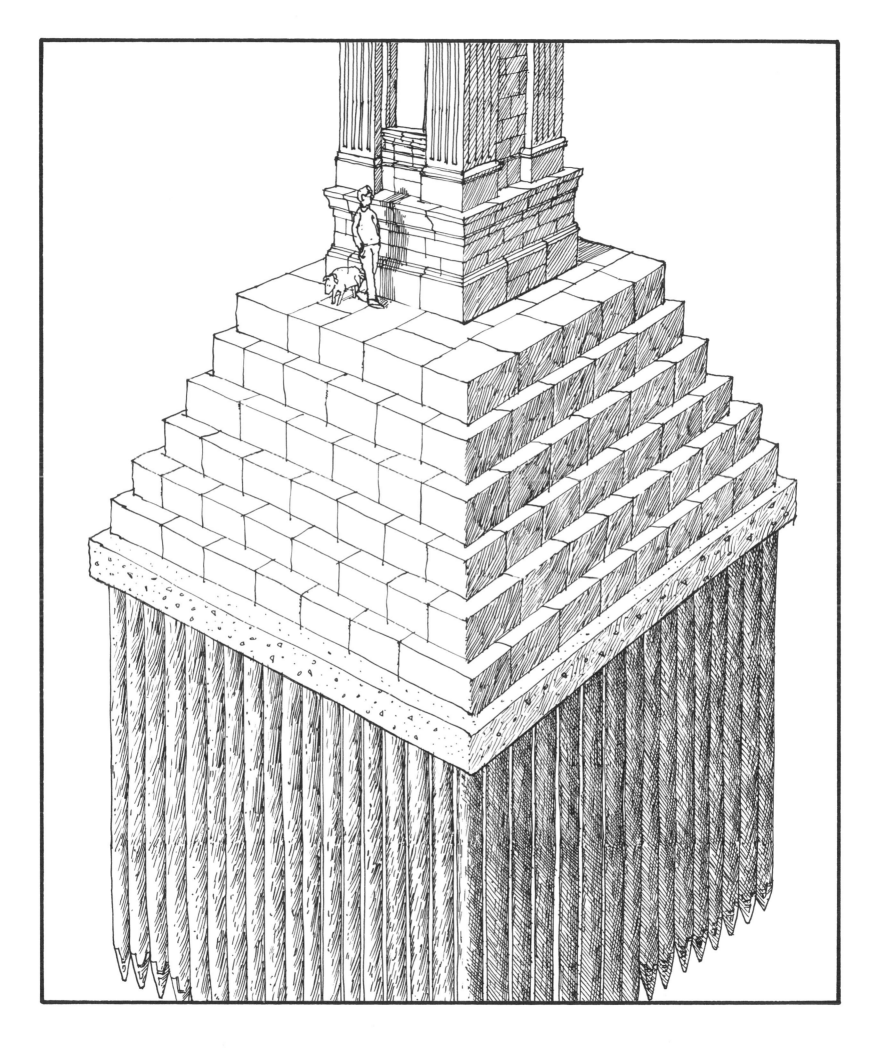

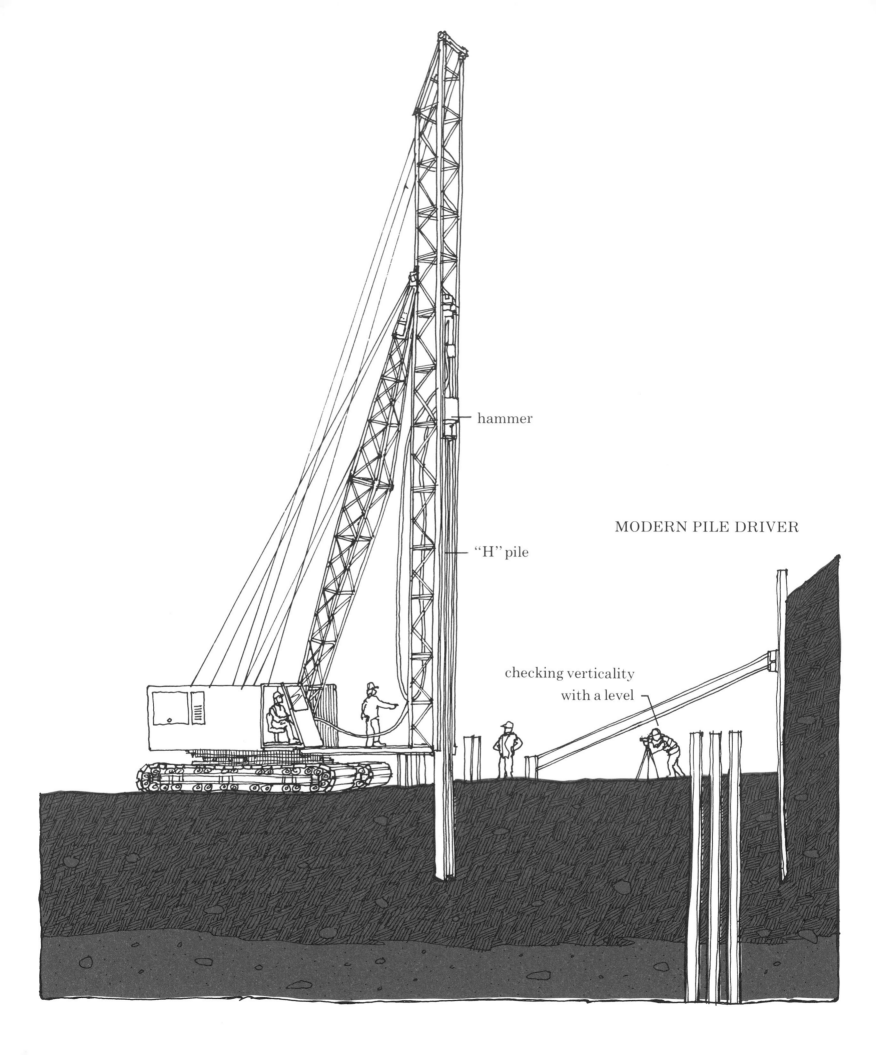

hammer

"H" pile

MODERN PILE DRIVER

checking verticality
with a level

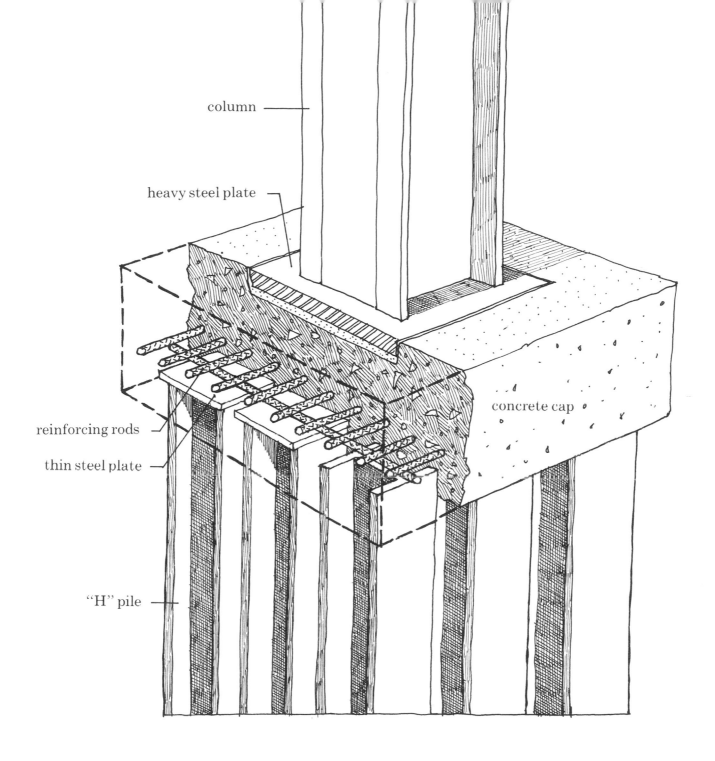

column

heavy steel plate

reinforcing rods

thin steel plate

concrete cap

"H" pile

Building number three stands on clusters of "H" piles driven to bedrock. Once the excavation has been completed, the rows of columns are accurately laid out on the site to insure that they will line up. As each section of pile disappears into the ground another is welded to it until the necessary depth is reached. When all the piles of a particular cluster are in place, the ends are cut off at the same height and the cap constructed. At the same time, a footing is laid out around the perimeter of the excavation on which the concrete enclosure wall will be built. When the footings and caps in an area are finished, the basement floor is ready to be poured.

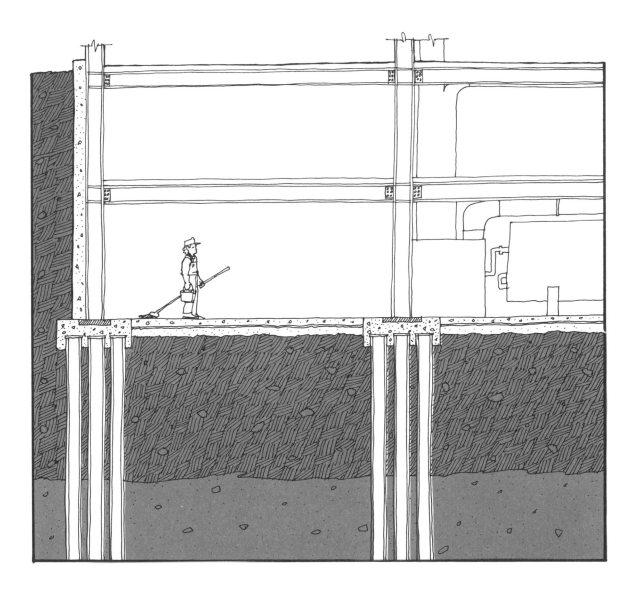

The remaining exposed soil is leveled and covered first with a layer of crushed stone and then with sheets of waterproofing plastic. Next, steel reinforcing rods are laid out and finally the concrete itself pumped into the area. As each section of basement floor is finished, the corresponding section of enclosure wall, any columns and floors below ground level, and any other miscellaneous concrete work is formed and poured.

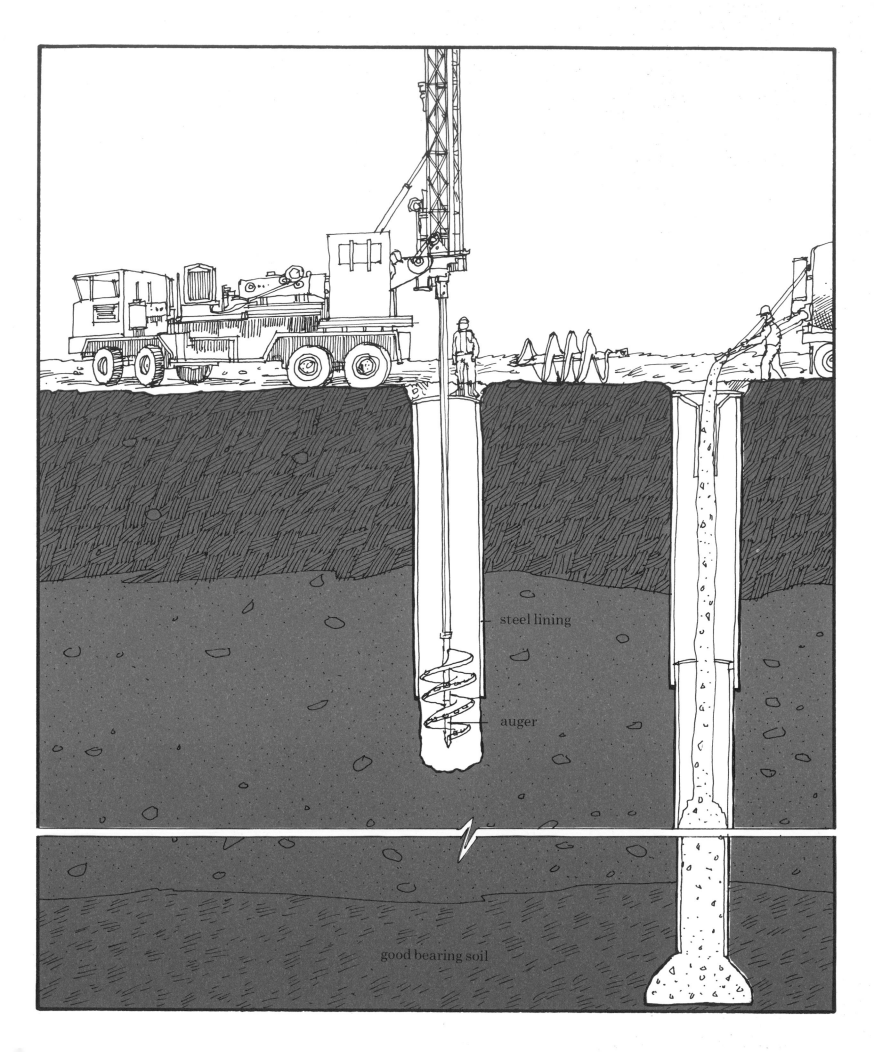

steel lining

auger

good bearing soil

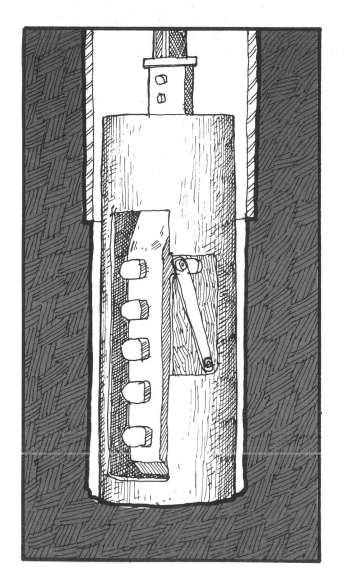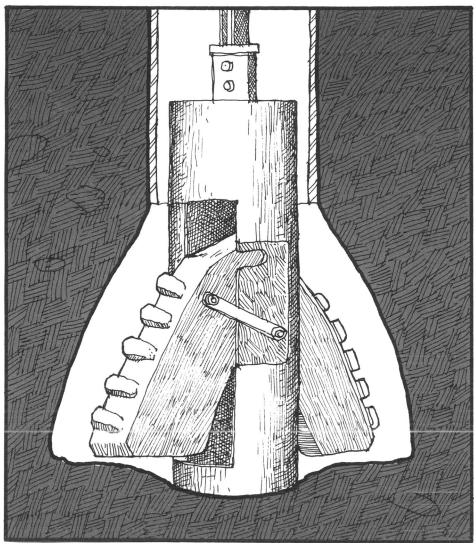

Once the pier locations for building number four have been marked on the site, a large hole is drilled at each by a circular cutting device called an auger. As the auger rotates, the space between its blades is filled with soil. It is periodically lifted out of the hole, bringing with it a core of dirt. As the hole is being dug, the lining, in this case a steel tube, is slid down inside it to prevent the soil from collapsing. When the top of the tube reaches ground level, a second, smaller tube, is slid down inside the first and the size of the auger reduced accordingly. This process is repeated as many times as the depth of the hole requires.

Because these piers will not go all the way down to rock, the bottoms are to be belled out. For this operation a special cutting tool that replaces the auger on the end of the drill is lowered to the bottom of the shaft. As it is rotated, a blade is extended from both sides to scoop out a bell-shaped cavity. When the bell reaches the necessary diameter, the shaft is filled with concrete. As it is being poured, each of the liners is removed, beginning with the smallest. As the concrete reaches the top of the pier, reinforcing rods are inserted.

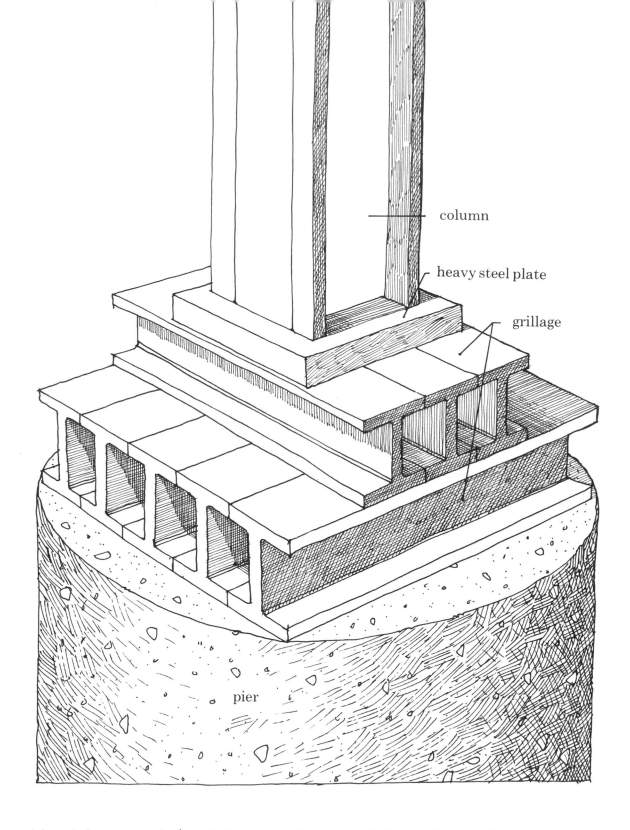

column

heavy steel plate

grillage

pier

After it has set, a layer of short steel beams is tied into the reinforcing. A second row of beams is placed above it and at a right angle to it. The steel work is called grillage and acts like a steel plate to distribute the load from the column more evenly over the top of the pier. The grillage is eventually covered with concrete as the rest of the underground work is completed.

While the space directly beneath a building contains the systems required to support its structure, the area under the surface of the streets and sidewalks is filled with the systems essential to support its occupants. The basic systems, which we call utilities, include water, sewage removal and drainage, electricity, steam, gas, and telephone communication.

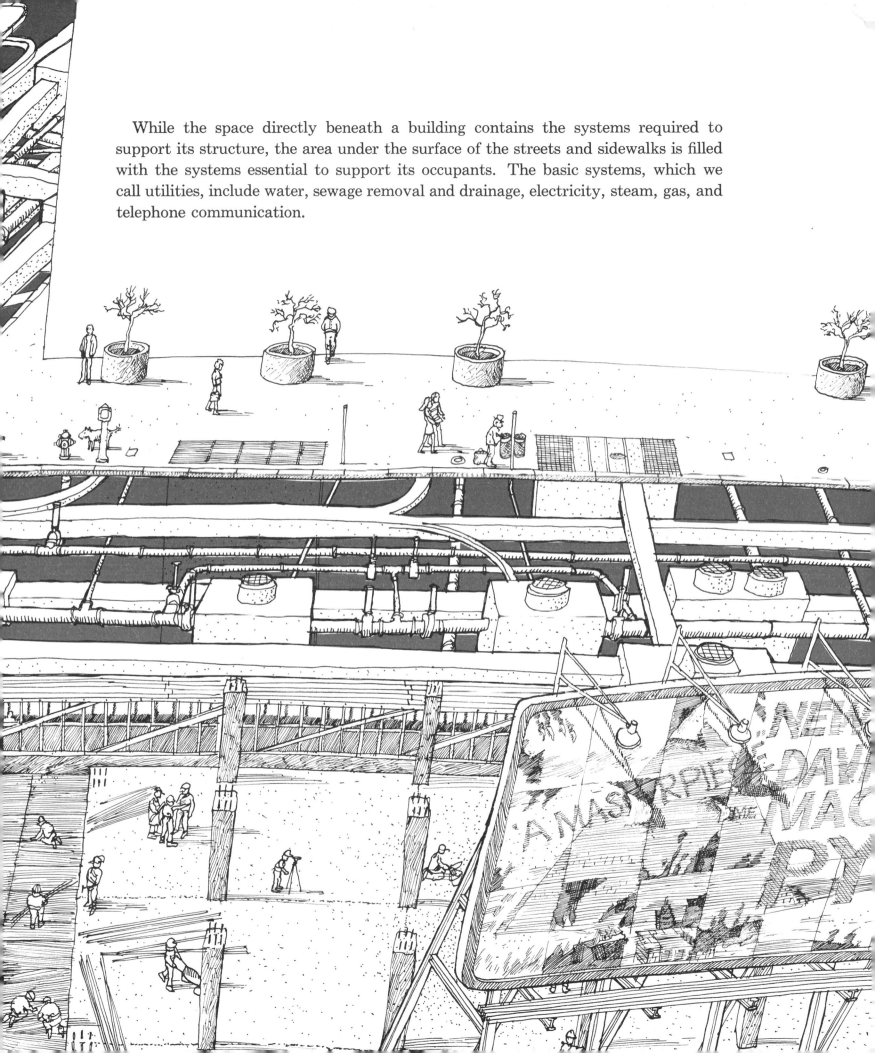

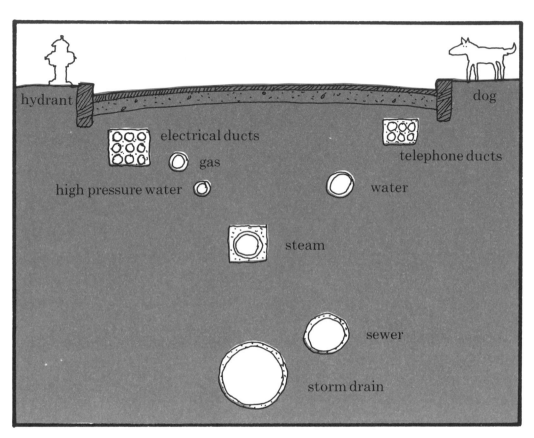

hydrant

electrical ducts

telephone ducts

gas

high pressure water

water

steam

sewer

storm drain

dog

## IDEAL UTILITY LAYOUT

When a new street is being laid out, each utility is given a specific location according to a master plan. The sewer and drain are located farthest down and approximately under the center of the street. Above them is the steam system, which needs at least six feet of soil above it because of the high temperatures it produces. Closer both to the surface and to the sides of the street are the water and gas pipes, while just two feet below the surface are the electric and telephone cables.

In an area requiring all these utilities, however, it is very rare that a new street can conform completely to this ideal plan. Most underground systems have grown gradually and randomly over many years and since the problem is usually to increase or replace what already exists, it is often necessary to squeeze things in wherever they will fit.

valve

HIGH PRESSURE SYSTEM

manhole

main

REGULAR PRESSURE SYSTEM

fire hydrant

submain

branch line

WATER SUPPLY SYSTEMS

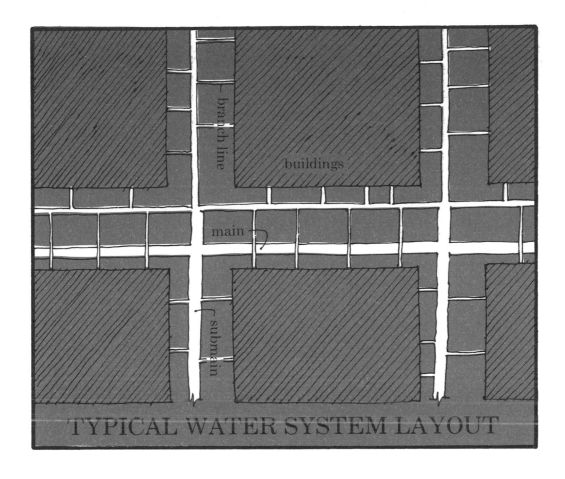

branch line

buildings

main

submain

TYPICAL WATER SYSTEM LAYOUT

One of the most important requirements in any city is the construction and maintenance of an adequate water supply system. Water, which is collected in distant reservoirs, is carried into a city's storage tanks through pipes and tunnels often hundreds of feet below the surface. To maintain a constant flow, both are situated, whenever possible, at a particular slope called a grade. If at any point enough of a grade cannot be achieved, the water must be pumped. Because of the size and complexity of the pipe systems within a city, it is impossible to rely on gravity to move the water. To insure complete distribution throughout the city a constant pressure is maintained in the pipes by continuous pumping. Most of the water is kept under low pressure and it serves the industrial, commercial, and domestic needs of the area. A separate high-pressure pipeline is often maintained to all fire hydrants where at any given time a large amount of water must be immediately available.

The largest water pipes under the street, called mains, are made of concrete, steel, or cast iron. They carry water from centralized pumping stations into predetermined districts of the city. Smaller pipes, called submains, are connected to the mains and carry water down each street. The smallest pipes, called branch lines, connect the submains to the plumbing systems within each building.

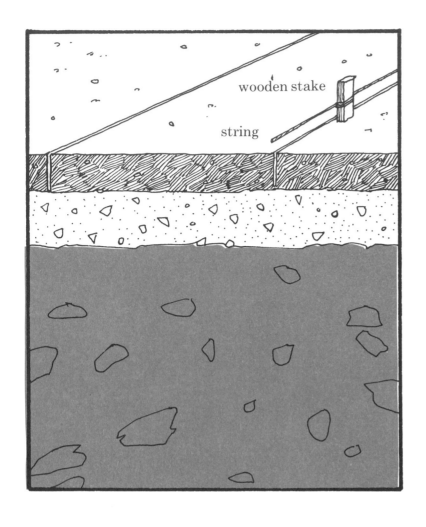

wooden stake

string

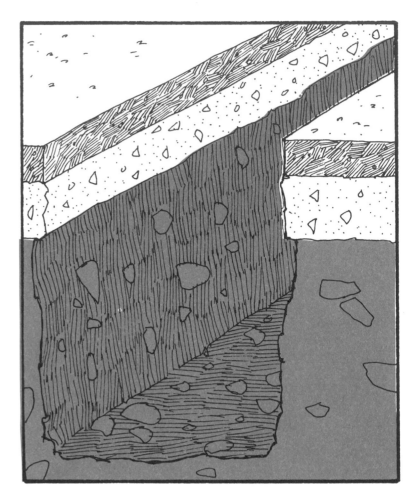

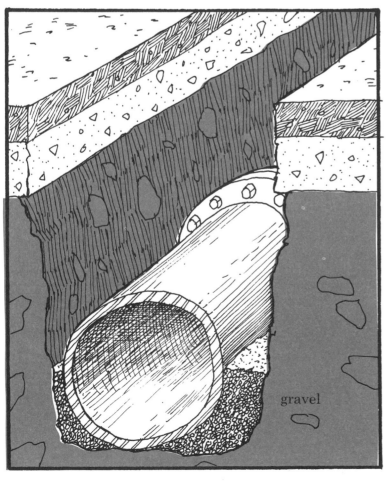

gravel

Once the location of a water pipe has been determined, the outlines of the trench in which it will rest are marked on the street surface. The asphalt and concrete roadbed between the lines is then removed and the trench dug to the required depth. All water pipes are buried in the ground below the frost line. This is a level about four feet below the surface above which the soil is likely to freeze. The trench is kept as narrow as possible so that a minimum amount of fill will be needed once the pipe is laid. The more fill used around the pipe, the more chance there is of excessive settlement.

As a section of pipeline is completed, it is carefully tested. If all the connections are found to be watertight, gravel is carefully packed around the exposed portions of the pipe and the remainder of the trench filled with soil. All pipelines are laid out as straight as possible to reduce the increased friction that arises when water is forced through sudden curves.

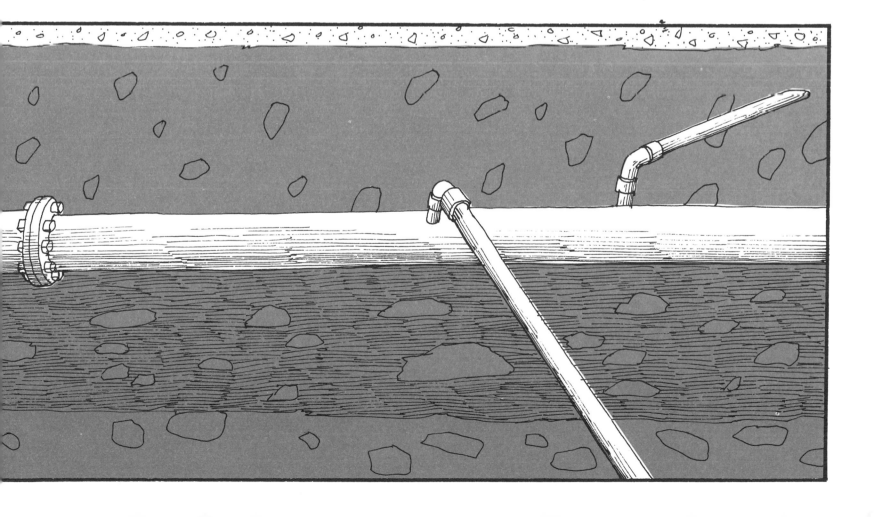

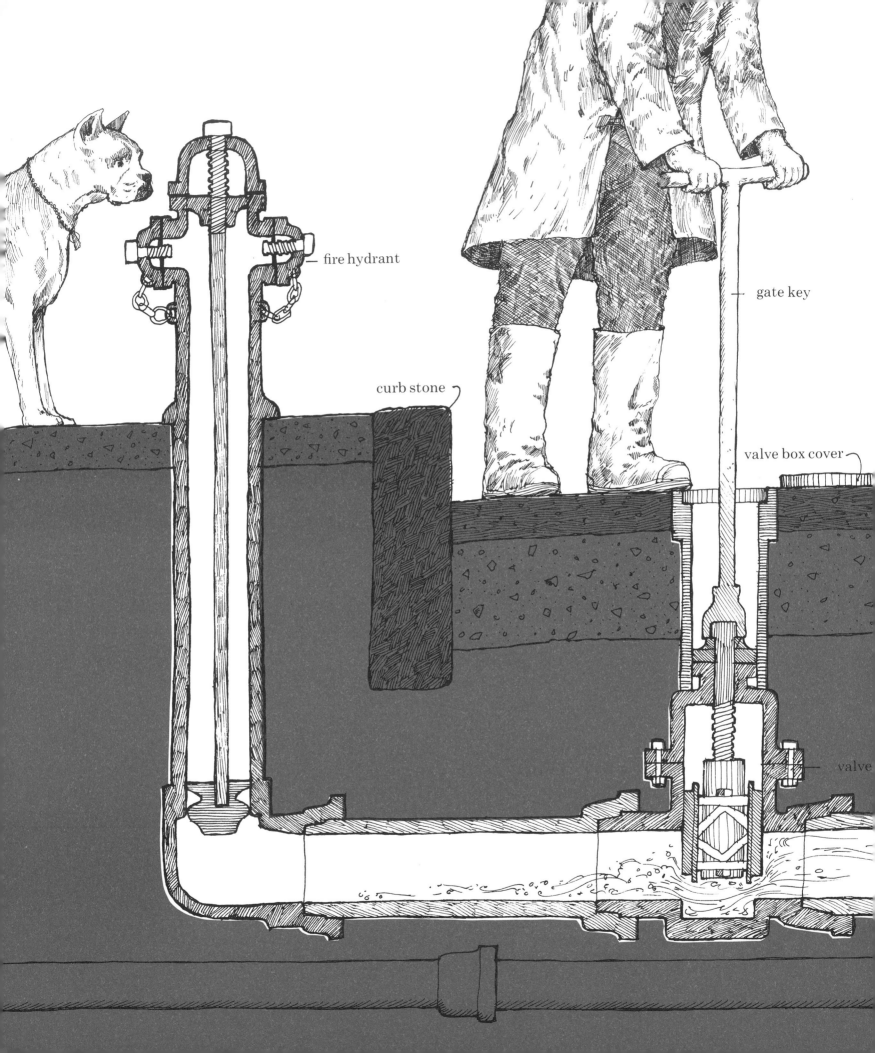

fire hydrant

gate key

curb stone

valve box cover

valve

Metal gates, called valves, are located inside the pipes, enabling a section to be shut off and repaired without closing the entire system. In the straight runs of pipe, they are located approximately every eight hundred feet, and at the intersection of three or more pipes they are located within each pipe. They are also located on all branch lines between the submains and the buildings. On top of each valve is a nut that is reached through a small opening in the street or sidewalk called a valve box. Each valve box is covered by a small square or round cast-iron lid. Valves are opened and closed by turning the nut with a long-handled wrench called a gate key. Other valves called air valves, which are located at high points along the pipeline, allow any trapped air to escape without releasing water.

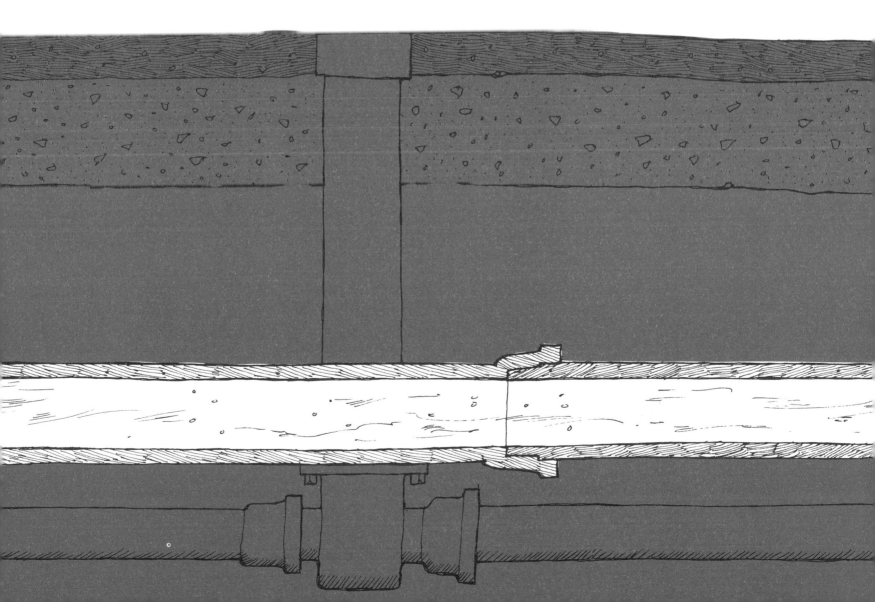

If a valve is very large, it is usually placed in a small room underneath the street called a manhole. This room is entered through a circular opening in the top, which in turn is covered by a cast-iron lid called a manhole cover. A manhole used in water supply or removal systems is usually about nine feet high and cylindrical with the upper portion shaped like a cone. Its walls are constructed of curved concrete blocks or bricks built up in layers or courses from a concrete floor slab. The cover fits into a cast-iron ring called a frame, which is set on the last course, reaching the level of the street.

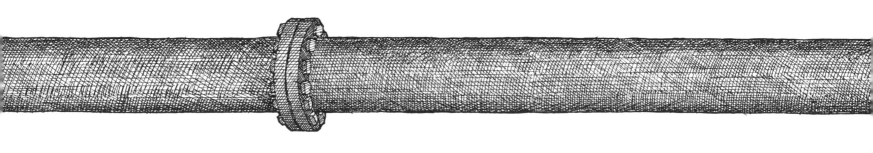

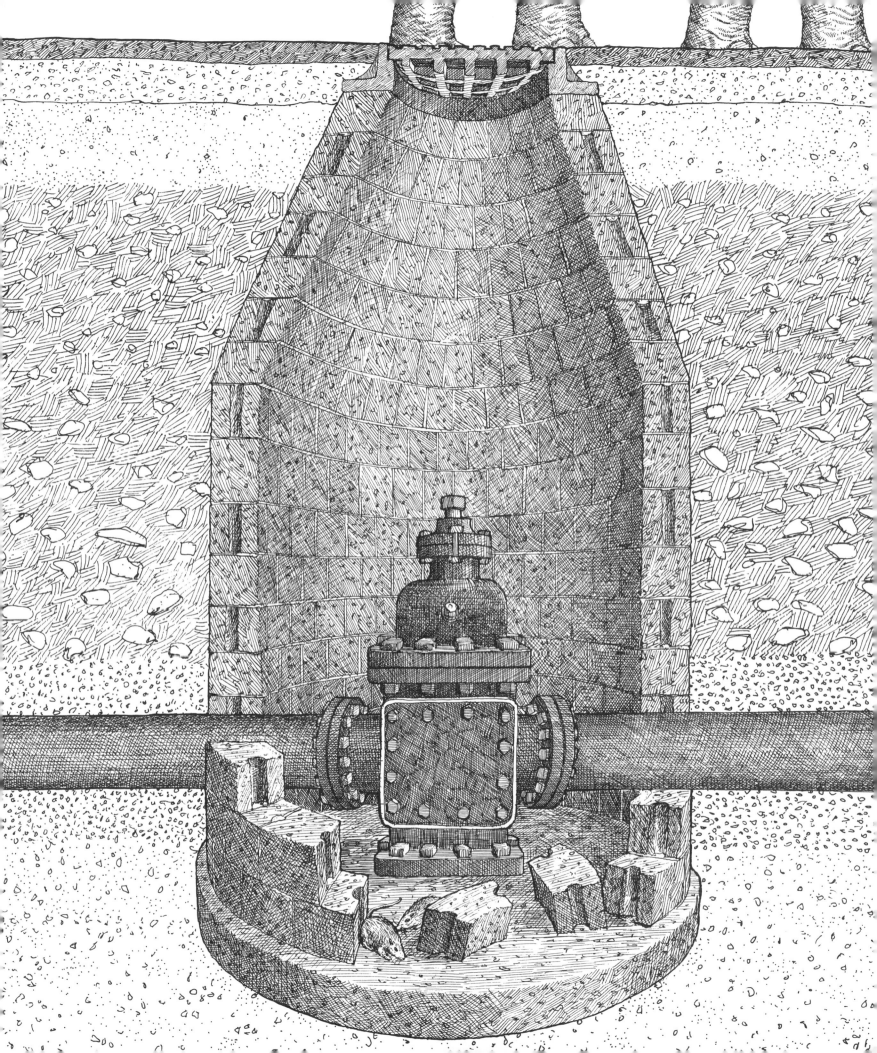

submain (clay)

manhole

main (concrete)

lateral

SEWER SYSTEM

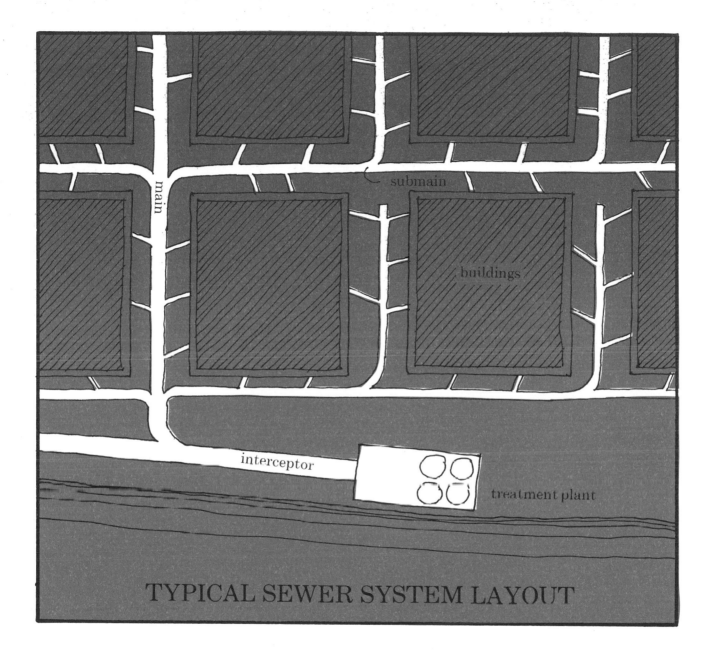

**TYPICAL SEWER SYSTEM LAYOUT**

If a system is constructed for bringing water into a city, another system must be built to remove the dirty water and waste, which is referred to as sewage.

Sewage from several buildings is carried through individual pipes into a larger pipe called a lateral. Several laterals are then connected to a submain, several submains to a main, and several mains to an interceptor. This is the largest pipe in the system and carries the sewage to treatment plants for cleaning.

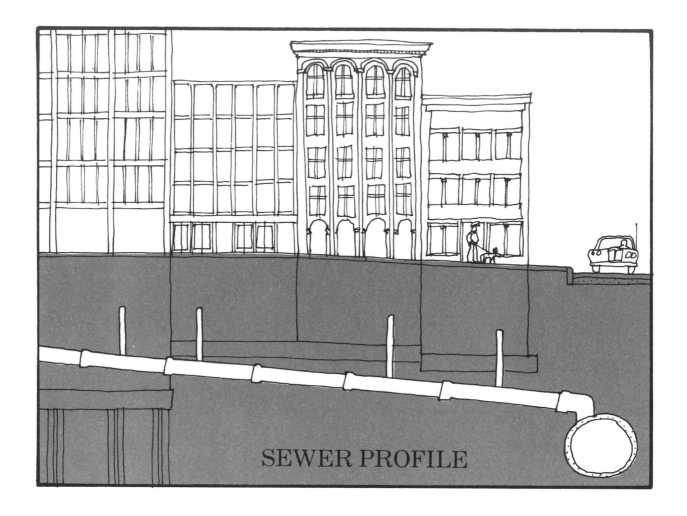

SEWER PROFILE

Unlike the water system, the sewer system relies almost entirely on gravity flow. For this reason a profile of every single street under which a sewer pipe will travel must be drawn to insure the correct grade and direction of that pipe. Sewer pipes are usually ten feet or more under the street, and they are always located well below the water pipes. This reduces the possibility of a leak from the sewer, which could contaminate the water supply.

Sewer pipes come in many different sizes. Those below thirty inches in diameter are often made of clay, while those larger are concrete. Clay is used because of its great resistance to the chemical action of the sewage. In both cases, the pipes are made with one end slightly larger than the other so that the narrow end of one section can be inserted into the wide end of the next continuously along the length of the pipeline. Because clay pipes are not as strong as concrete pipes they are often supported on a bed of concrete. As a section of pipeline is finished, it is carefully inspected and tested before the trench is filled.

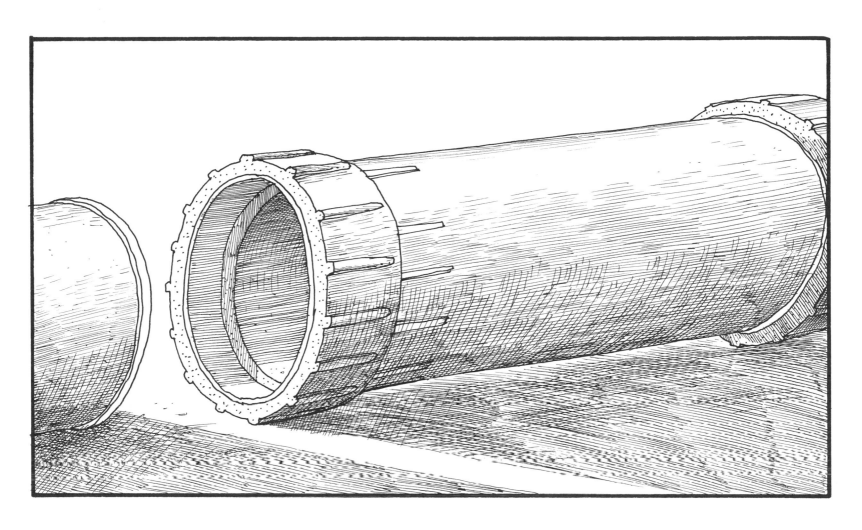

At each major change of direction or grade in the sewer system, a manhole is constructed, providing a point from which the pipes can be cleaned. When the sewage from two submains is to pass into a main, all the pipes are connected to a manhole. Open curved channels in the floor of the manhole lead the sewage with a minimum amount of friction from one pipe into the next.

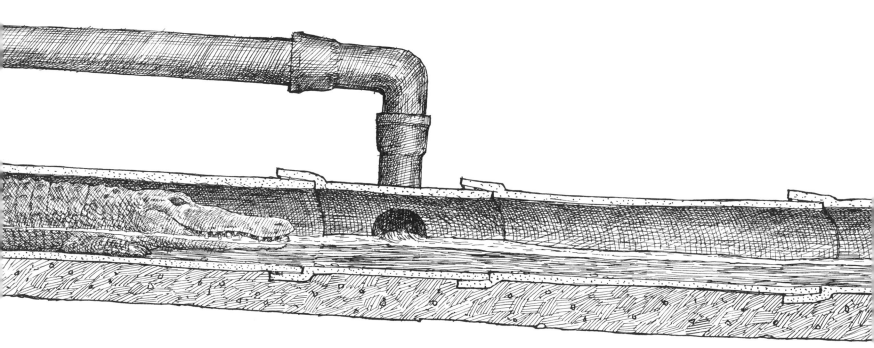

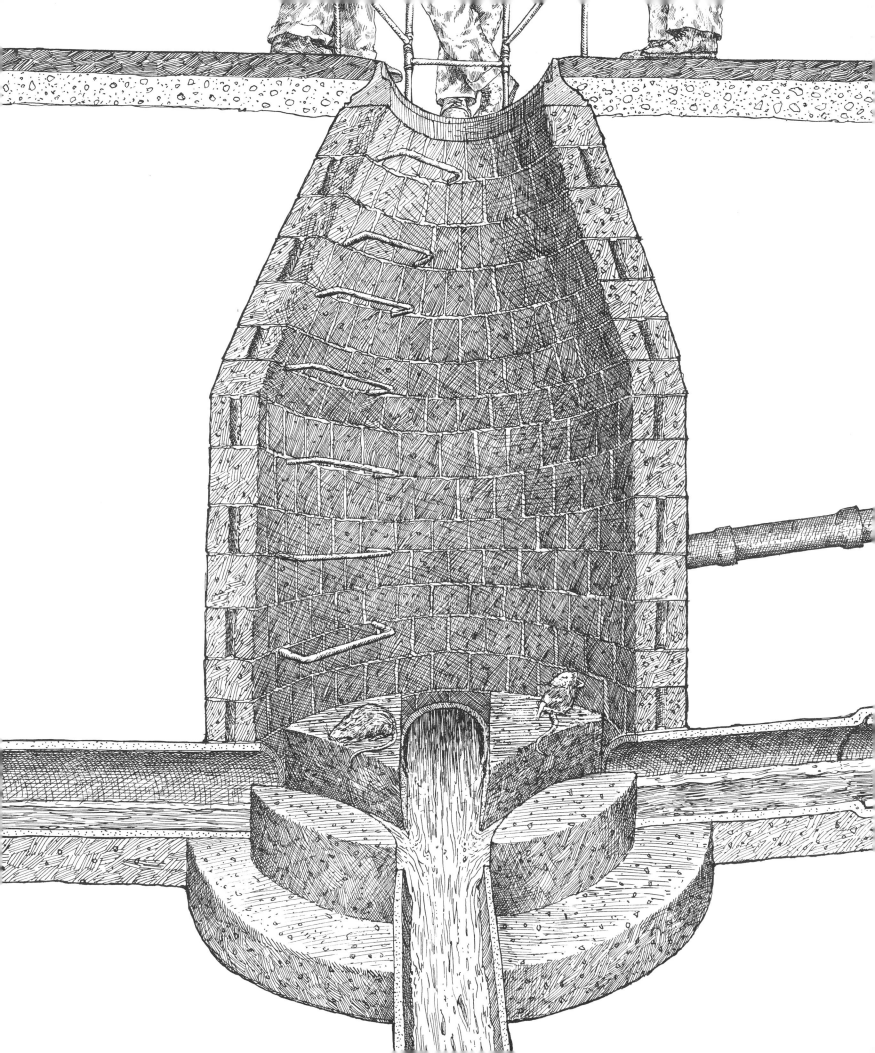

catch basin

inlet

STORM DRAIN SYSTEM

A second system, sometimes combined with the sewage system, is the network of storm drains. These pipes carry away large amounts of water that sometimes accumulate very quickly from a storm or melting snow and that otherwise might flood basements, manholes, and subways. These pipes can easily be ten times the size of a sewer pipe and are usually located below all the other utilities. Many of the old storm drains were made of brick but now they are usually constructed of concrete. Water flows into the storm system through inlets, catch basins, or a combination of the two.

An inlet is a hole in the street or curb covered by an open, cast-iron grate. The surface of the street is carefully graded to channel water through the grate and into the pipe, which connects directly to the storm drain. A catch basin is a rectangular storage tank located under the street. Not until water reaches a certain height in the tank does it enter the pipe connecting to the drain. By creating this delay, any

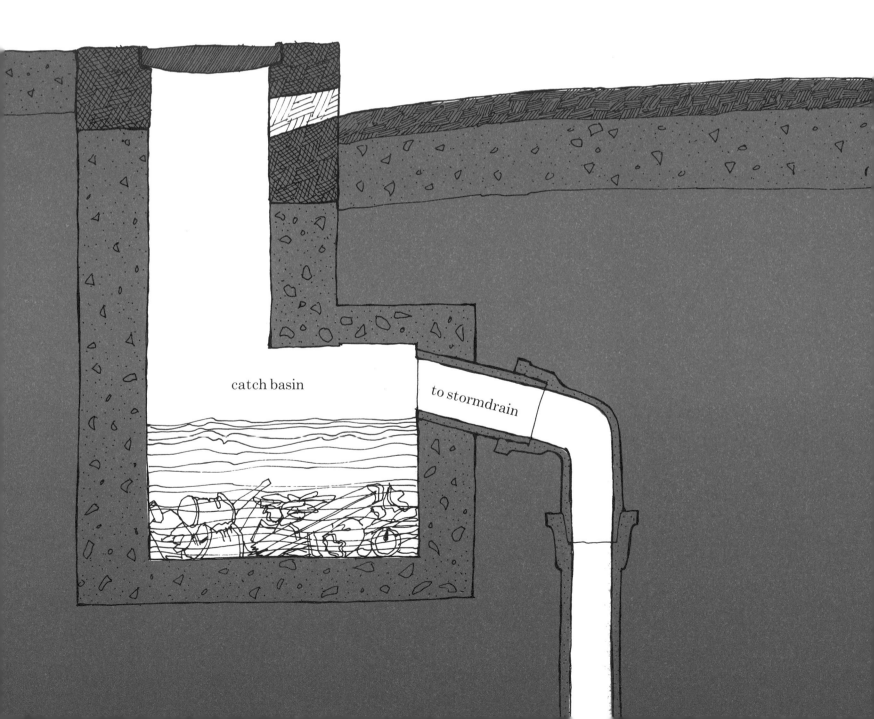

catch basin

to stormdrain

objects carried into the system that could clog the pipes have time to settle to the bottom of the catch basin. These objects are periodically removed through a circular opening above the catch basin that is otherwise covered by a round plate similar to a manhole cover.

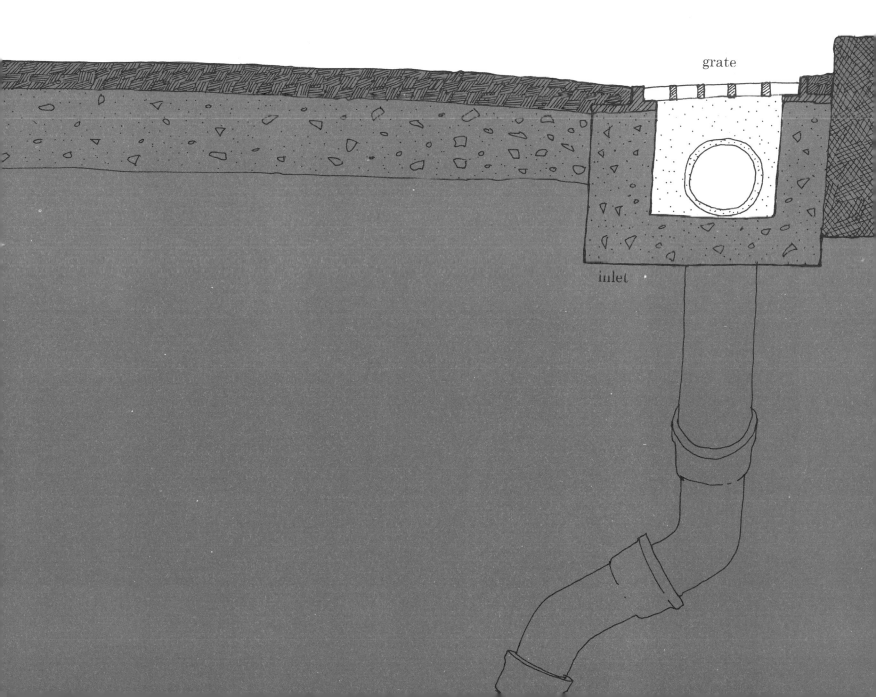

grate

inlet

transformer
vault

street light

ducts

manhole

old brick manhole with
drain to sewer

ELECTRICAL SYSTEM

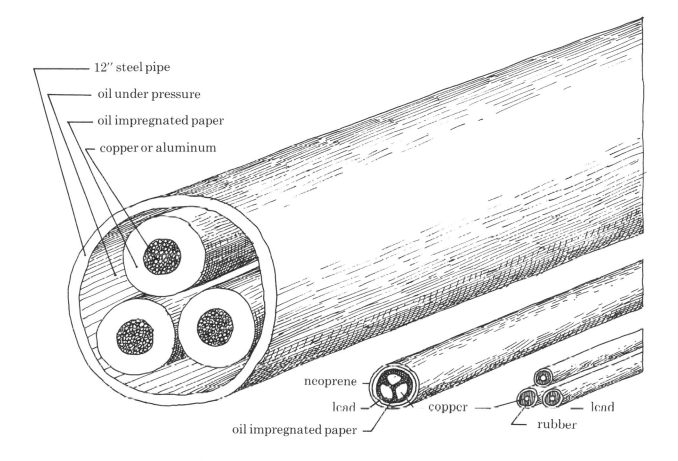

12" steel pipe

oil under pressure

oil impregnated paper

copper or aluminum

neoprene

lead

oil impregnated paper

copper

rubber

lead

Electricity is produced at large generating plants and carried through heavy-duty cables enclosed in pressurized steel pipes to transformer stations in different areas of the city. At each station the very high voltage from the main plant is reduced to meet the needs of each district. From there it is carried through smaller cables to other transformers, where the voltage is again reduced to satisfy the requirements of individual buildings. These last transformers are located in underground rooms, usually larger than manholes, called vaults. Along the route from the transformer station to the vaults manholes used in the installation of the cables are located under the street. Because cables are pulled underground from one manhole to another they are usually cut in maximum lengths of two hundred feet. In the manholes the end of one cable is fastened to the beginning of another.

Each cable is usually around two and one quarter inches in diameter and contains three separate copper wires. The cable is first wrapped with oil-impregnated paper, then with lead, and finally it is sealed in a rubberlike casing called neoprene. Each is located underground in a protective pipe called a duct. Several ducts are usually placed at the same time and are grouped into a rectangular cluster called a duct

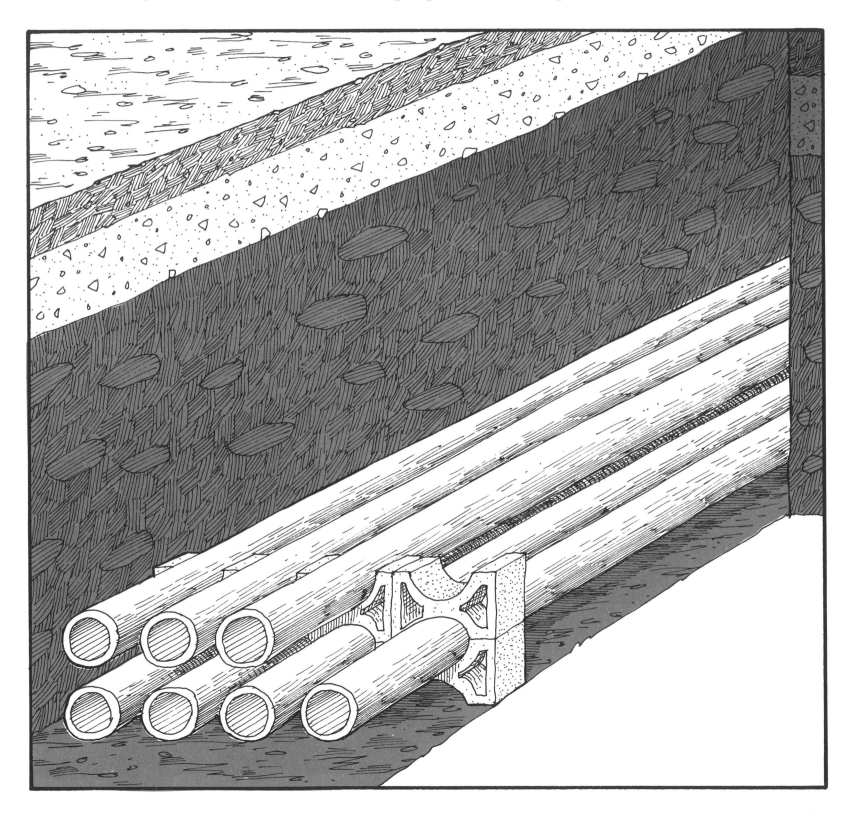

bank, which in turn is encased in concrete. For added protection, duct banks are placed in the street with at least two feet òf cover between them and the pavement. Ducts are placed in a trench, one horizontal row at a time. They are supported a few inches above the soil and about two inches apart to insure that the concrete will completely surround each one.

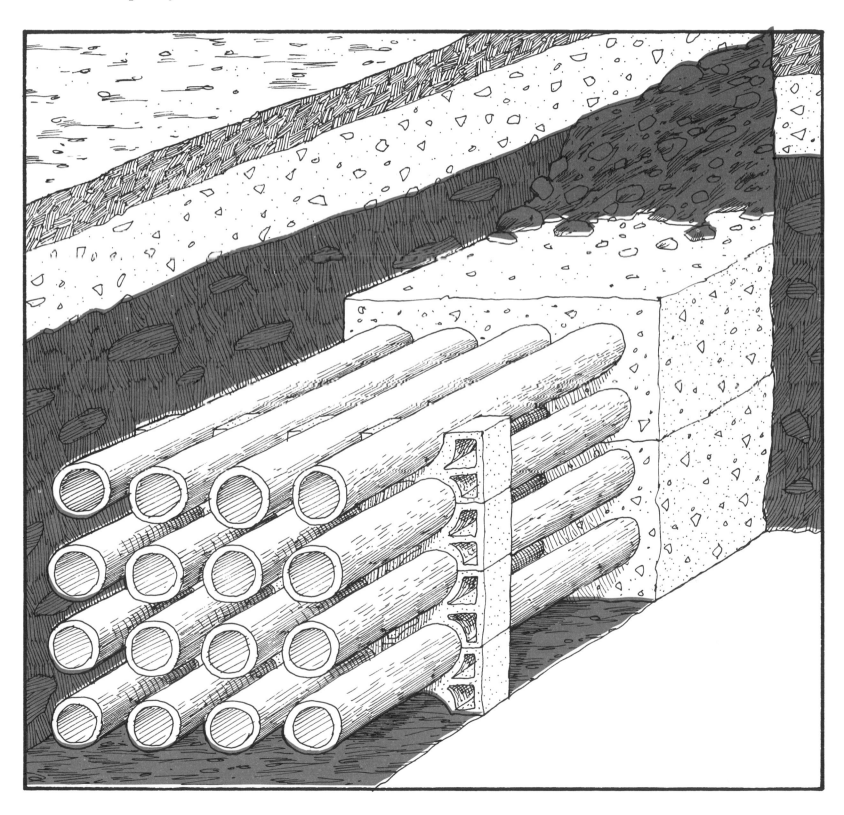

At both ends of a duct bank the pipes open into manholes. The average electrical manhole is rectangular and about thirteen feet long, five feet wide, and six feet high. They are made of reinforced concrete either formed and poured on the site or precast and brought to the site ready to be lowered into a hole. In either case the floor slopes gradually toward a small recess called a sump pit. Water that collects in the manhole will flow into the pit and can be more easily pumped out. An electrical manhole is entered through a concrete enclosure on top called either a chimney or a neck. The cast-iron frame and cover rest directly on this enclosure.

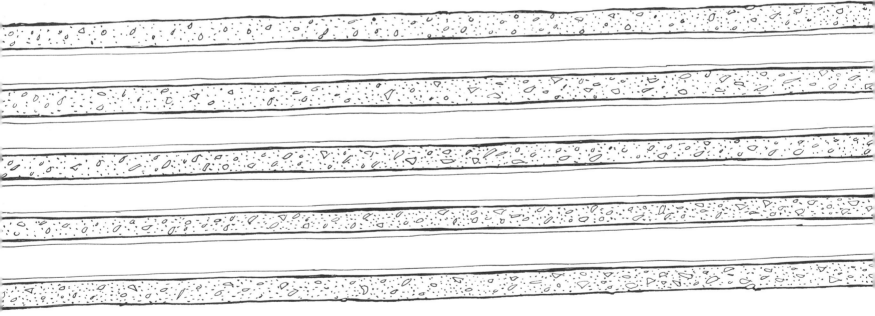

Once the manhole, and all necessary ducts connecting it to other manholes, vaults, and street lights are finished, the soil is packed in around them and a new road surface laid. At this point the cables themselves are pulled. From the first manhole a nylon or steel line is either shot with air pressure or simply pushed through the entire length of a duct. At the second manhole the end of the line is fastened to a steel rope, which in turn is fastened to a powerful winch. The winch, a machine that will mechanically wind the rope, is located in a specially designed truck parked above the hole. The rope is then pulled through the duct into the first manhole.

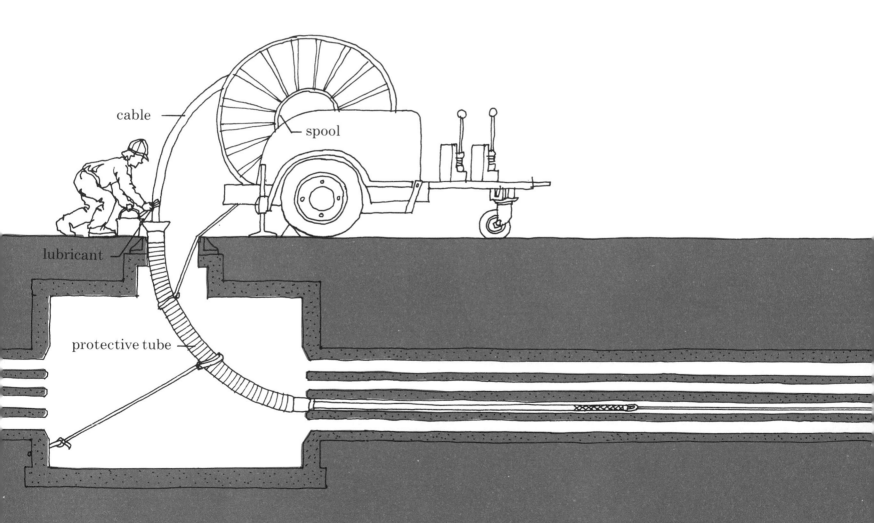

cable

spool

lubricant

protective tube

PULLING AN ELECTRICAL CABLE

The electrical cable, which is wound around a large spool, is then fed through a protective flexible tube into the manhole and secured to the end of the steel rope. Both the flexible tube in the first manhole and the rope in the second are secured in such a way as to insure as straight a pull as possible to reduce friction. A special lubricant is smeared on the cable as it enters the tube. While the winch turns, pulling both rope and cable through the duct the pressure is continually checked to avoid stretching or weakening of the cable's covering.

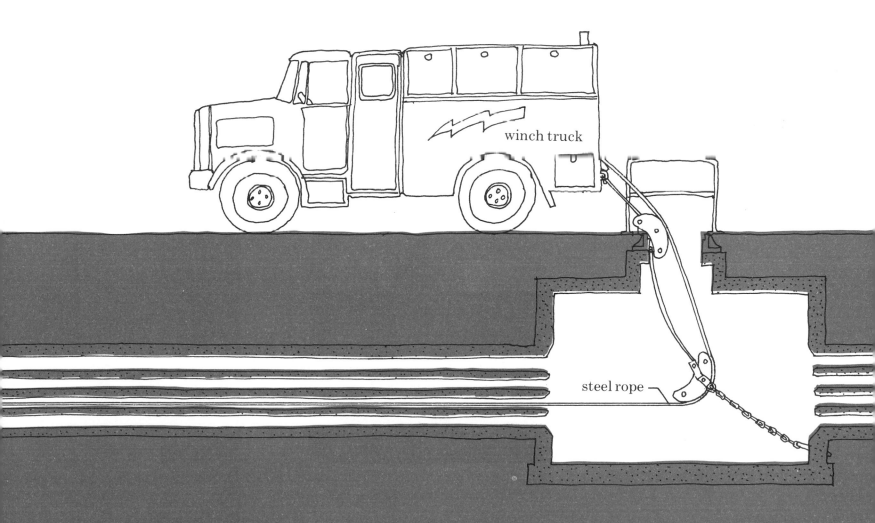

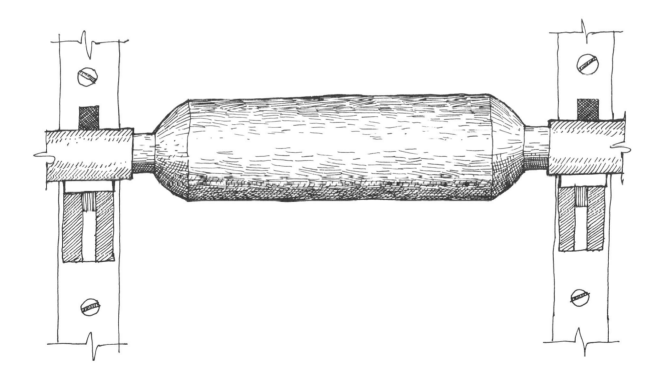

In the manholes both ends of the cables are supported against the walls on projecting metal brackets called racks. As two cables are joined together the connection is wrapped with tape and then encased in a lead sleeve. Once sealed, the sleeve is checked for leaks by forcing air into it.

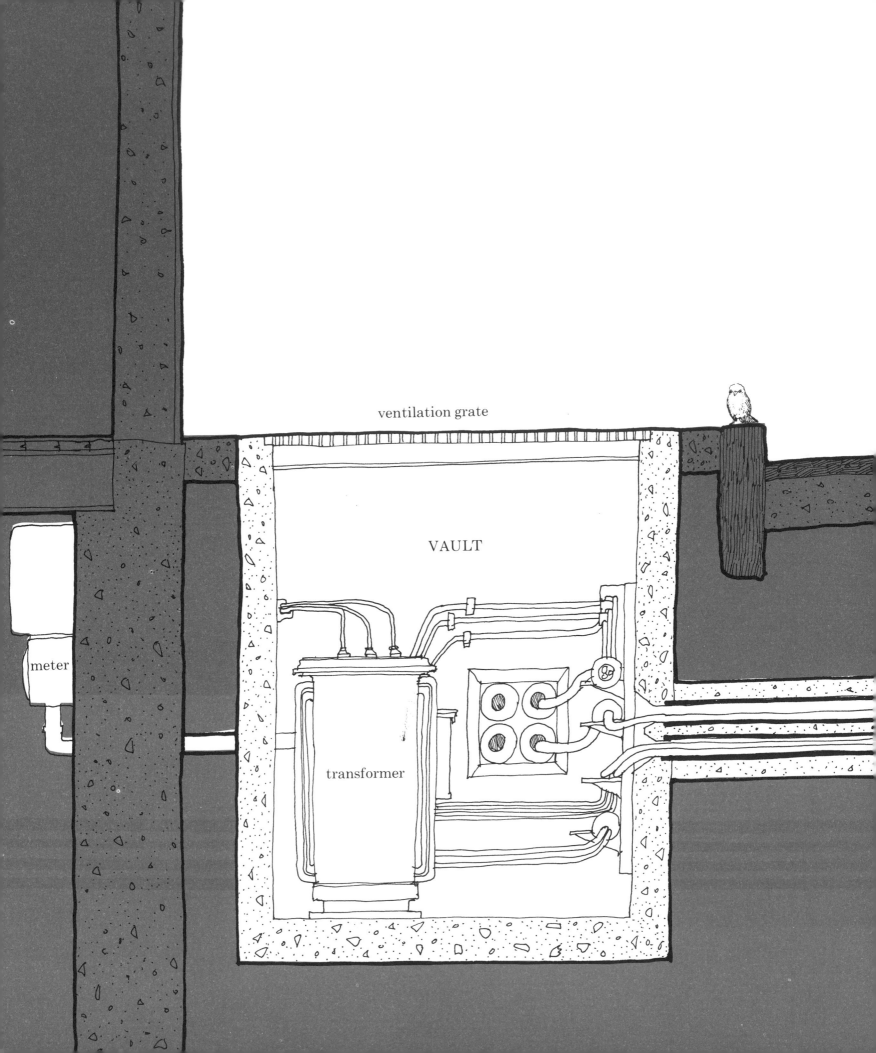

ventilation grate

VAULT

meter

transformer

Besides cables, a manhole might also contain a small transformer. In a situation where a building uses a lot of electricity a transformer just for that building is often placed in a vault under the sidewalk in front. Vaults are often partially covered with an open steel grate, allowing ventilation of any heat produced by the transformer. As all electric cables enter buildings, the current passes through a meter, which measures and records the amount consumed.

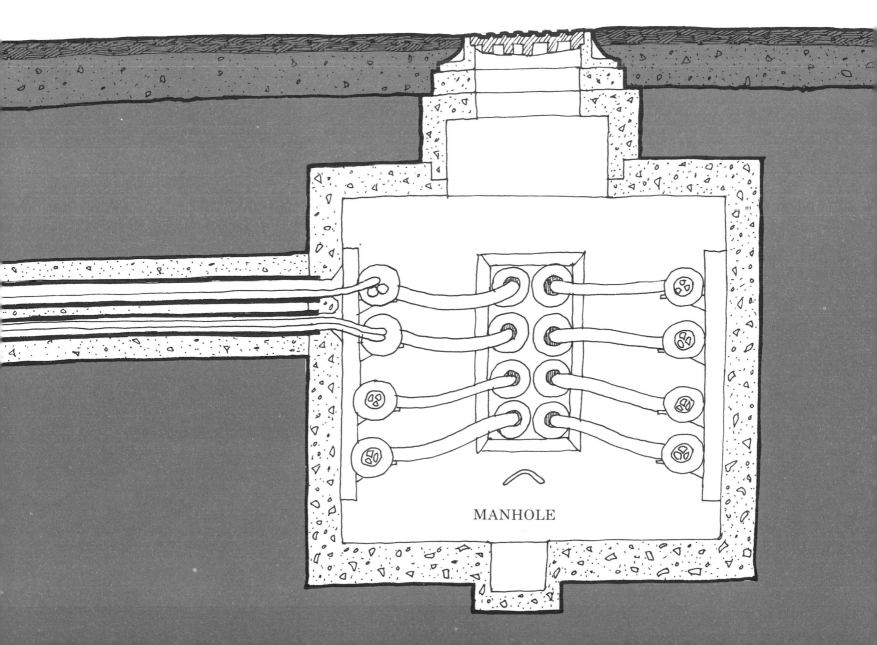

MANHOLE

drain to sewer

STEAM DISTRIBUTION SYSTEM

Besides providing electricity, it is not unusual for an electric company to also provide steam. The first steam piped into a city was merely a by-product of the electrical generators and came therefore from the main power plants. Now, however, power plants exist in many cities for the sole purpose of producing steam. Steam is fed under pressure into a system of mains, submains, and service pipes. The mains and submains are two-inch-thick welded steel pipes, the largest of which are twenty-four inches in diameter.

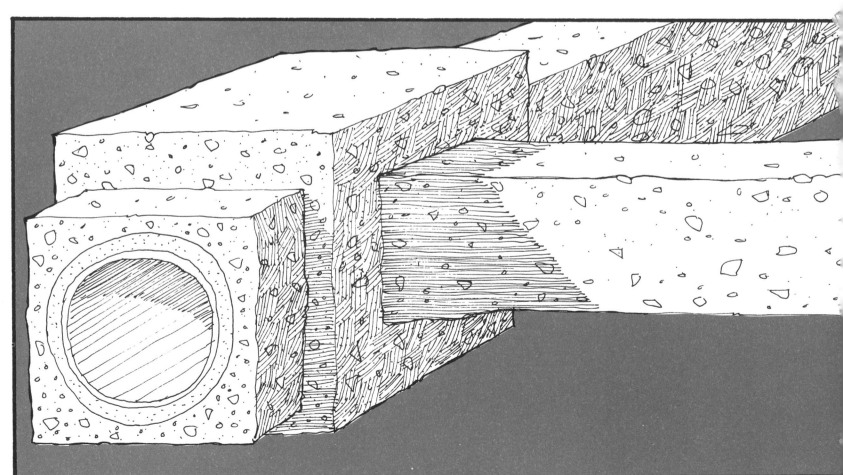

Because of possible damage to other utilities from the heat, steam pipes are usually buried at least six feet below the surface and encased in concrete. The trench, which will act as a form for the concrete, is dug only a few inches wider and deeper than the pipe itself and the floor is carefully graded for drainage purposes. The sections of pipe are set on supports about six inches off the ground and welded together. Each connection must be absolutely airtight and is therefore x-rayed. Not until the x-rays are checked is the pipeline approved. At specific locations, steel straps called anchors are welded around the pipe. These will be permanently embedded into the concrete. Approximately every hundred feet, flexible connections called expansion joints are inserted between sections of the pipeline. They allow for expansion or contraction in the pipe due to changes in temperature. The entire pipeline is then wrapped in a two-and-a-half-inch thick coat of insulation, and the concrete itself is poured until a minimum of four inches covers the top of the pipe. The trench is widened slightly around the anchors and expansion joints to increase the thickness of the concrete at those locations.

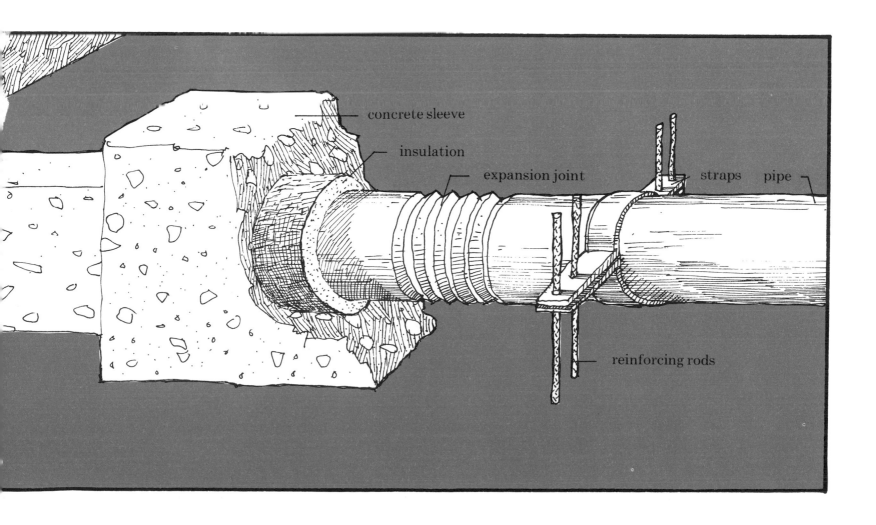

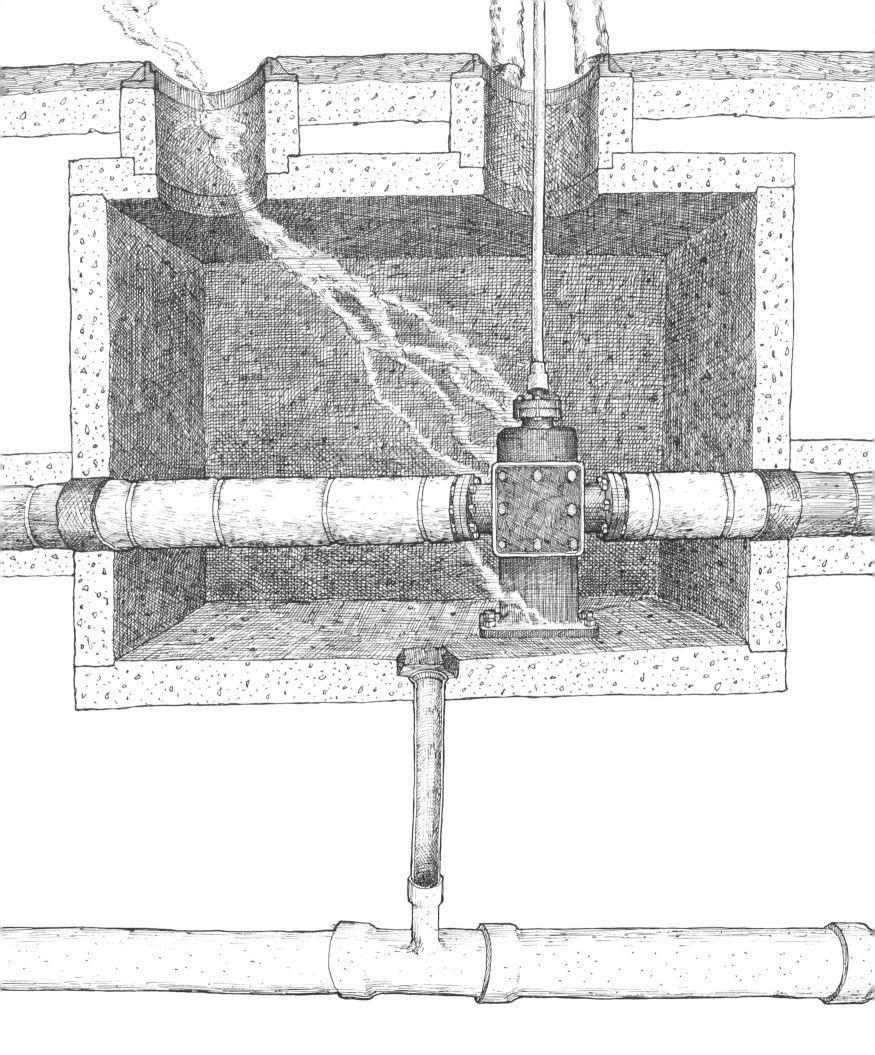

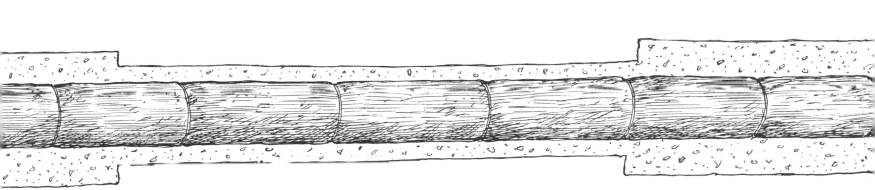

As in the water system, the distribution of steam is regulated by a series of valves and meters reached either through valve boxes or manholes depending on the size. Most steam manholes are rectangular and have two entrances from the street. This allows for more efficient exhausting of hot air by pumping fresh air into one hole and allowing it to escape through the other. Small amounts of moisture that collect between the pipe and the concrete liner are channeled directly into nearby sewer lines. Water from broken water mains or heavy rains that remain around the lining for any length of time turns to steam and rises up through the first opening encountered whether it be a manhole, catchbasin, or crack in the pavement. If a lot of steam begins to rise from a manhole one of the covers is usually replaced by a six-foot-high sheet-metal chimney, which lifts the steam above both pedestrians and cars.

GAS DISTRIBUTION SYSTEM

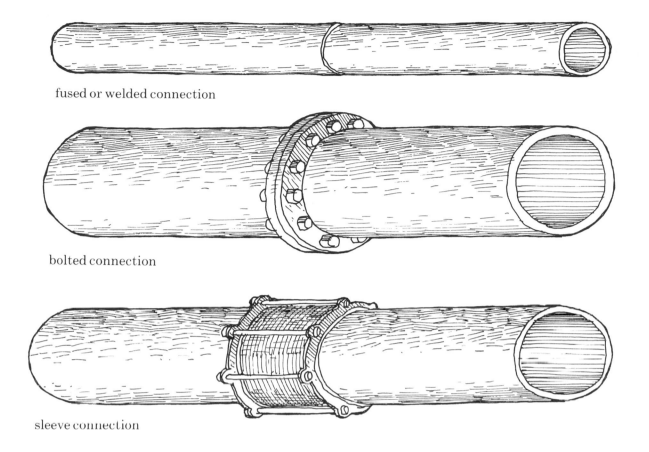

fused or welded connection

bolted connection

sleeve connection

Natural gas is another utility piped under the streets for heating and air conditioning as well as cooking. Natural gas is created and trapped in pockets hundreds of feet below the surface of the earth by the decomposition of organic matter. Shafts are drilled down to the pockets and the gas is collected and fed into large steel pipes called transmission lines. They often carry the gas hundreds of miles under great pressure to wherever it is needed. Natural gas can also be transported over land and water as a liquid simply by freezing it. Storage tanks for liquid natural gas can often be seen around a city's perimeters. No matter in what form it is delivered, natural gas at some point enters an underground network of distribution mains and service pipes. Both metal and plastic pipes are used to carry gas and both are placed a minimum of three feet below the street. If the pipes are steel or cast iron, they are bolted, welded, or linked together by a special sleeve that fits over the joint. Once the connections have been tested, the soil is carefully packed in around the pipe. If plastic piping is used, the ends are heated and fused together. When the seams have been checked, the space around the pipe is packed with sand over which the regular fill is then placed.

The success of a gas distribution network depends on the maintenance of specific pressures within the different pipes. This is accomplished by installing checkpoints throughout the system. Each checkpoint consists of two concrete manholes located about twenty-five feet apart. The same distribution main runs through both. Connected to the main in each manhole is a device called a regulator. This device is controlled automatically by pressure in the pipe and can increase or reduce the flow of gas as required. Any particles of matter in the gas that could clog up a regulator are removed by special filters also in the manholes. Small amounts of gas that may be periodically released from a regulator are vented under the street to a six-foot vertical pipe on the sidewalk.

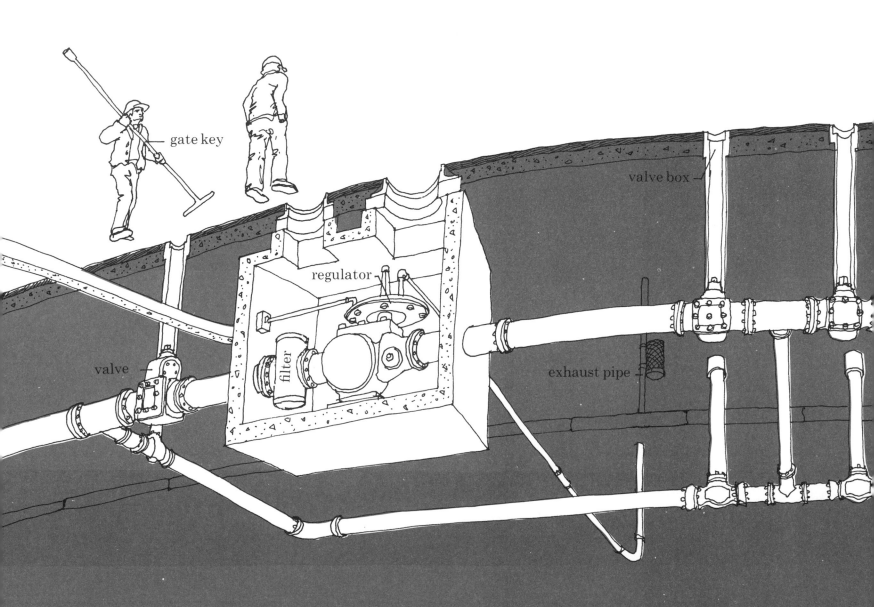

A second pipe, connected to the main before it enters the first manhole and again after it leaves the second, serves as a by-pass. Should a mechanical problem arise, the gas can be diverted around one or both of the regulators by opening or closing a sequence of valves on the by-pass and the main. These valves, as well as others located on the service pipes feeding all buildings, are usually placed under the street or sidewalk and reached through valve boxes. As an additional precaution to the regulators, the pressure in certain gas lines is monitored at a central control office. Electrical impulses are carried from the gas mains to gauges and alarms on the control panel through one of many underground telephone cables.

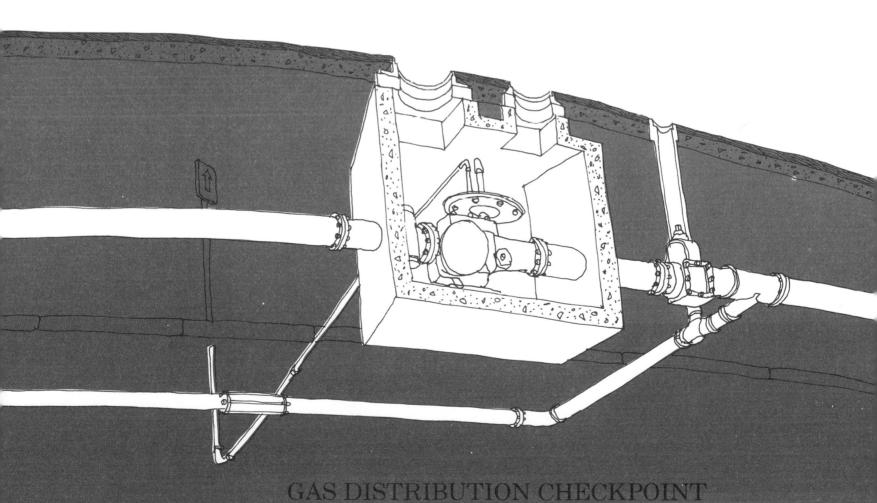

GAS DISTRIBUTION CHECKPOINT

telephone booth

traffic light

cross walk
signs

ducts

police telephone or
fire alarm

TELEPHONE SYSTEM

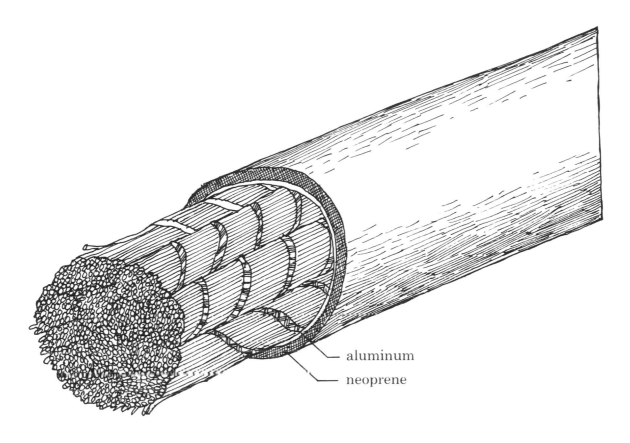

aluminum
neoprene

Each telephone call must eventually use two wires — one for the outgoing message and one for the response. For this reason thousands of wires are necessary in each system and an average underground cable contains 5400 wires or enough for 2700 simultaneous conversations. The cables are about three inches in diameter and are wrapped in aluminum and neoprene. The wires inside are grouped into clusters, each bound with a different color wire. Each individual wire within a cluster has its own unique marking.

If a wire has to be found for any reason, the repairman will first look up the number of the cable through which the wire travels. This will lead him to a specific manhole and duct location. Once the cable is opened, the correct color-coded cluster is identified and then the wire itself can be isolated from the rest.

While work is being done in a manhole, fresh air is pumped in through a large flexible tube. A high steel collar set into the opening prevents any small objects from falling into the manhole. Once the cables have been hung on the brackets or racked for easier access, the thousands of necessary connections are made. After the cables are joined the entire connection is encased in a lead or plastic sleeve, which is sealed and kept under pressure. A small tube, fastened to the sleeve, leads to a control panel. If a break occurs, the reduction in pressure triggers an alarm while the flow of escaping air prevents water from seeping into the cable until the break is found.

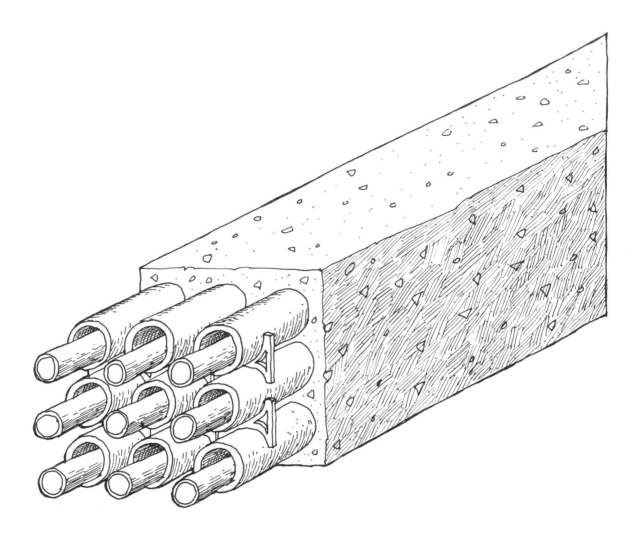

This particular function is only one of the many telephone communications within the city that passes through highly sophisticated equipment located in the central telephone office. In a few thousandths of a second, this equipment is activated by electrical impulses, either from numbers dialed, or as in the case of the gas line, from a change in the pressure, and automatically makes the connection between the wires of the incoming call and the wires to the required destination.

Calls made in the city travel through underground cables often laid parallel to and at the same depth as electrical cables. Once again manholes are constructed for pulling, connecting, and feeding cables into the buildings and phone booths. All the cables run through ducts, similar to electrical ducts, again grouped into clusters and encased in concrete. Cables from traffic lights, fire alarms, and police telephones also run through telephone company ducts but do not pass through the central telephone office.

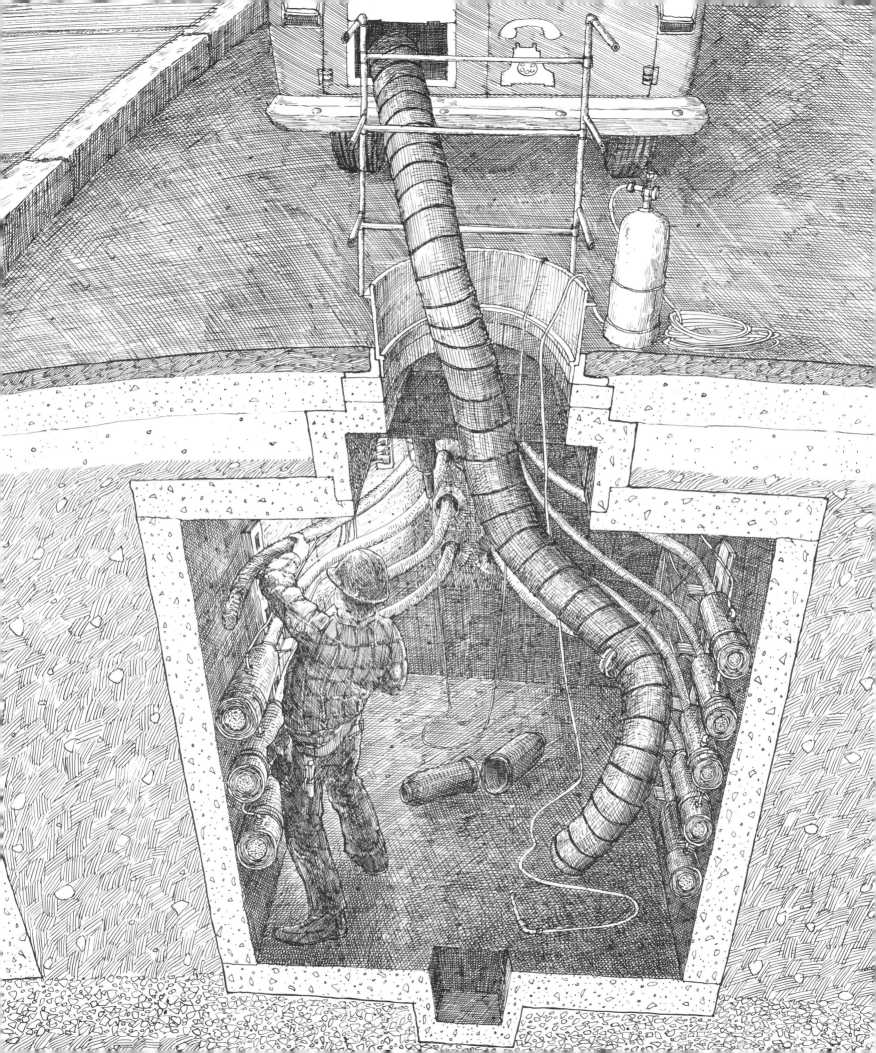

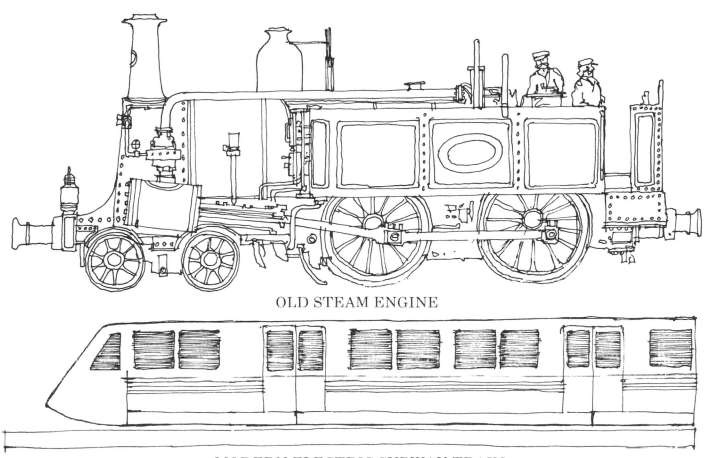

OLD STEAM ENGINE

MODERN ELECTRIC SUBWAY TRAIN

As a city grows and its population increases, the capacity of the utility systems must also be increased. This is basically achieved by increasing the number or size of the underground pipes and cables. But also as the size and population of a city grow, the need for an additional system — a fast and efficient means of transportation — becomes obvious. The congestion of vehicles and people, along with the often haphazard layout of the streets on the surface, has virtually forced this additional system underground.

The first underground train system was built in London in the middle of the nineteenth century. The engine itself was powered by steam. Since then a variety of electric-powered, high-speed subway systems have been developed and are in use in cities around the world.

The route and depth of a subway system is determined mostly by the needs and limitations on or just below the surface. But the choice of route must also take into consideration the locations of storage and maintenance areas for the equipment and for the power stations necessary to run it.

"cut and cover" tunnel

There are two basic types of tunnels used in subway systems. The first, because it is quite close to the surface, is limited to a location under existing streets and open spaces. It is constructed by the "cut and cover," method which we have already seen many times. This involves digging a trench, constructing the tunnel in the trench, and filling in the leftover space when it is finished. The second type of tunnel is actually bored through the ground and can therefore extend much deeper. This type of tunnel is used when there can be no disruption at street level or when the subway must pass under such obstacles as buildings, rivers, and other subways. When the route for either type has been selected, a plan is drawn indicating the precise locations of all utilities, existing subways, types and depths of foundations, and soil conditions along it.

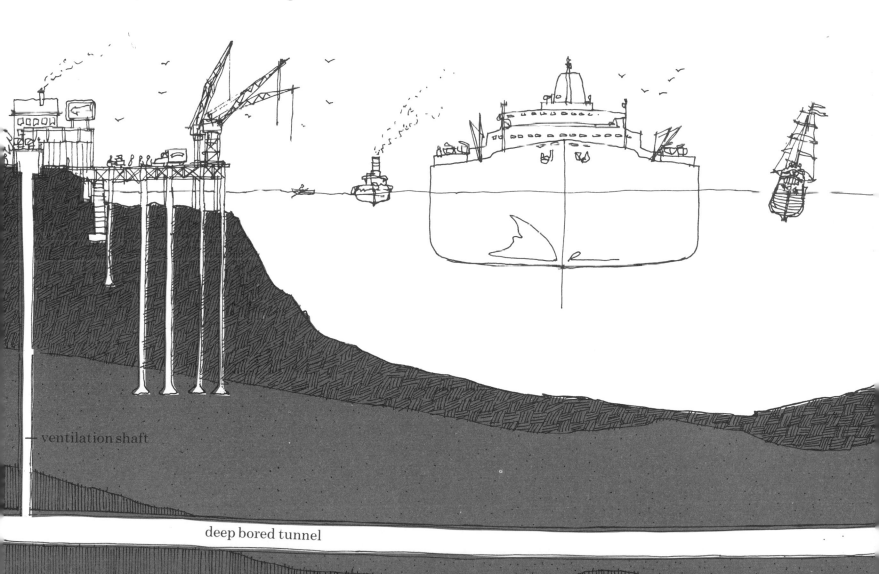

ventilation shaft

deep bored tunnel

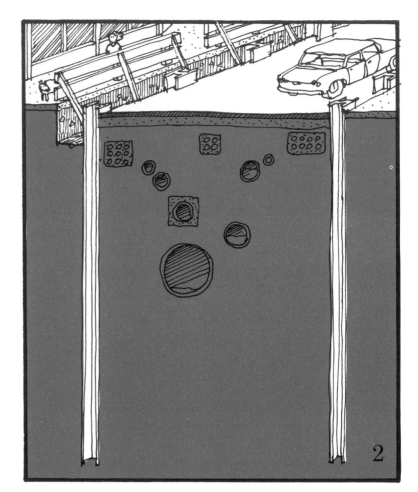

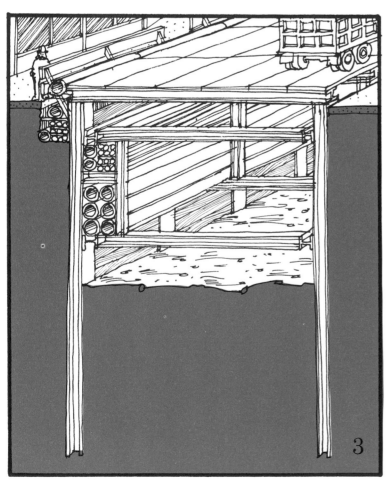

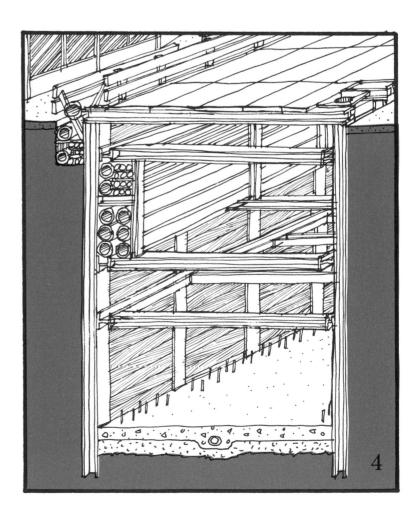

"Cut and cover" construction is carried out one or two blocks at a time to minimize disruption of surface traffic. The utilities are either diverted and fed into temporary pipes and ducts along one side, or they are supported on horizontal shoring, or they are suspended from the temporary roadway that will cover the trench.

Once the location of the outer walls of the excavation are marked on the street, soldier beams are driven. When they are in place, heavy steel beams that will span the trench are set down on top of them. Between them is placed a layer of twelve-inch-square wooden beams or thick steel plates, creating not only a temporary road for regular traffic but also a bridge from which material and equipment will be lowered into the excavation. When the roadway is finished, the soil below is carefully removed, exposing all the utilities. Once they have been safely supported or diverted, the remainder of the trench can be dug fairly quickly. When the floor of the trench has been prepared, the necessary formwork for the floor and the walls of the tunnel can be erected. A drainpipe is placed under the floor between the track locations. At predetermined low spots in the system, any water that accumulates will be pumped into the nearest sewer. All cables needed for running the subway either for power, signal, or emergency systems, will be pulled through ducts built into the wall. A vault is located every few hundred feet along the tunnel, for this purpose.

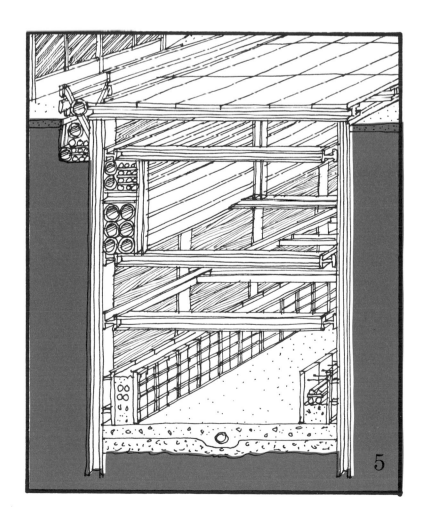

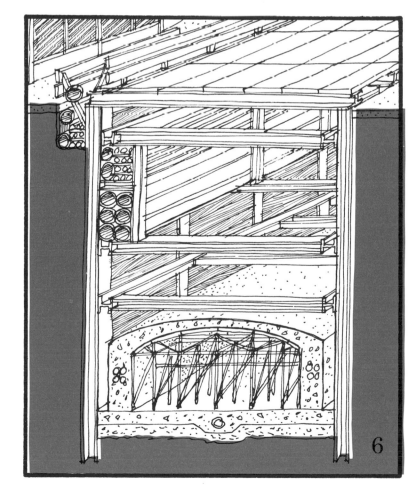

When the reinforcing rods are in place, the concrete is poured from street level through long funnels. When the walls are finished, the formwork for the roof is supported between them on heavy scaffolding. As soon as the roof is finished, the tracks, lighting, and signaling system are installed. When the outside of the tunnel has been waterproofed, the trench is filled with compacted gravel and soil. As the height of the fill reaches the appropriate level, each of the utilities is returned to its original location. New manholes are built wherever necessary and then as a new roadbed is constructed, the temporary road is dismantled. Vertical sections of the trench are permanently enclosed with concrete walls to serve either as escalator wells and stairwells or as ventilation shafts.

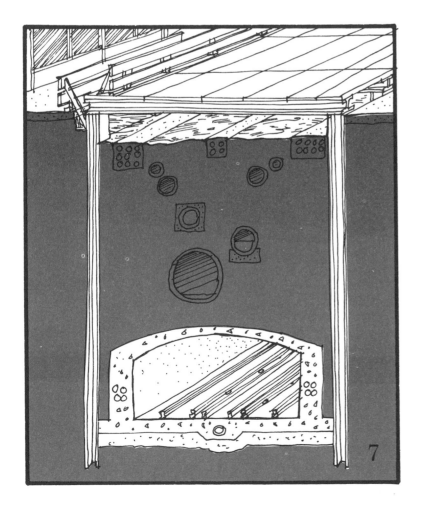

7

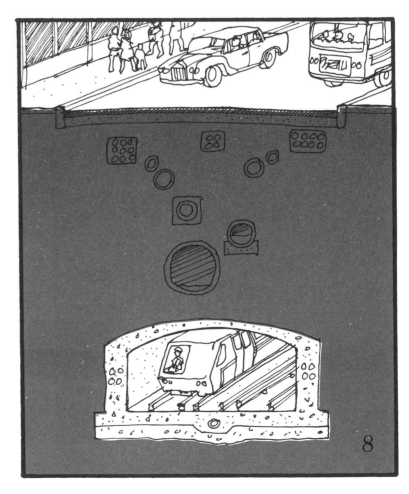

8

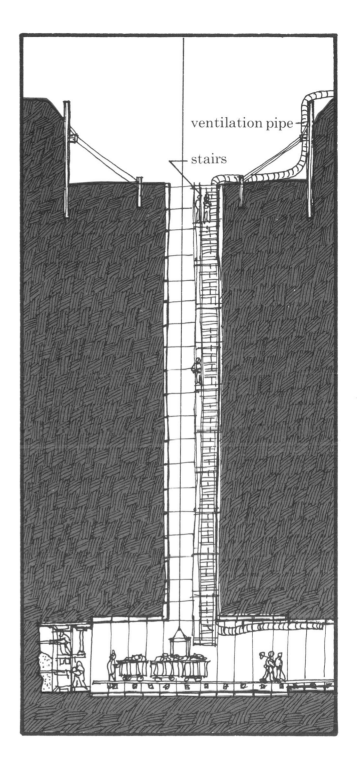

The process mostly used for boring deep tunnels involves digging a series of vertical shafts to the required depth at intervals along the route and connecting them together. The shafts, which allow access to the work area for men, materials, and fresh air, also provide a means of removing the soil and rock, called muck, produced by the excavation. As the shafts are sunk, they are lined to prevent collapse of the soil and reduce water seepage from the surrounding area.

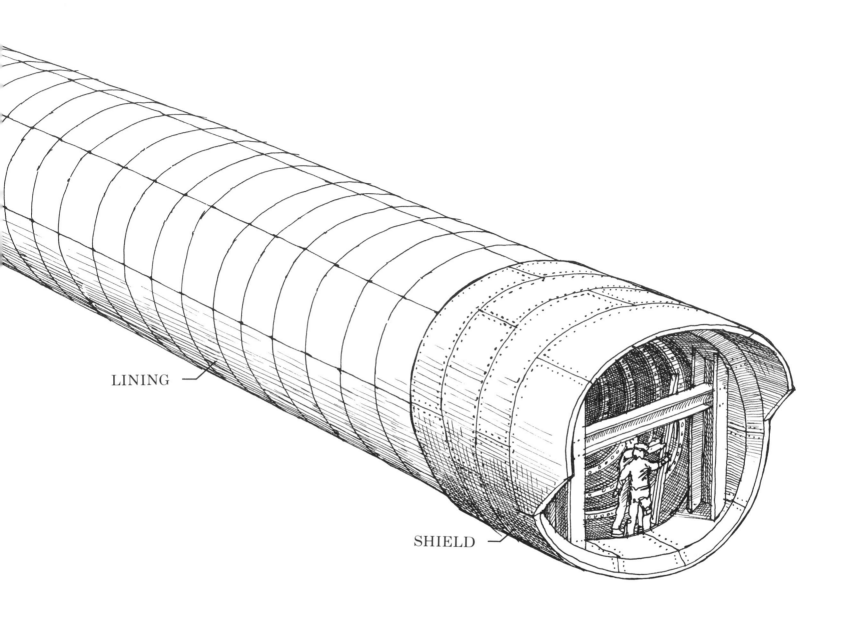

LINING

SHIELD

When tunneling through clay or unstable rock, a steel tube, called a shield, which is slightly larger than the intended diameter of the finished tunnel, is used. The shield is lowered in pieces down a shaft and assembled in a specially tunneled work area either in line with or adjacent to the proposed train tunnel. The top of the shield at the end nearest the excavation or face, as it is called, is extended to prevent loose material from falling into the work area. At the other end of the shield, called the tail, workers install the cast-iron or precast concrete liners that create the finished inner surface of the tunnel. Each cylindrical section of liner is composed of several segments.

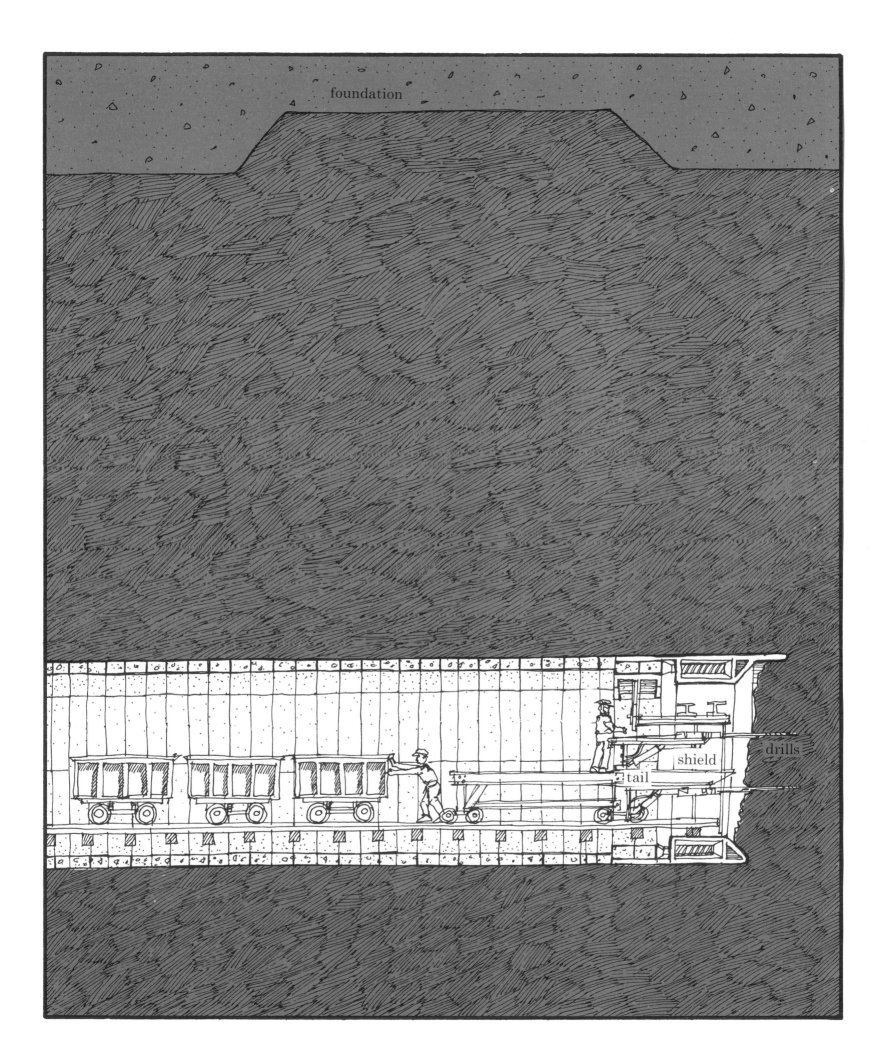

foundation

drills

shield

tail

As each two or three feet of the face is excavated, the shield is pushed forward with powerful jacks braced against the closest section of lining. As the shield moves, it leaves a small space between the actual surface of the soil and the outer face of the liner. In the older linings this space is filled with a special concrete, but in the newer linings the segments are pushed directly against the soil as soon as the shield has

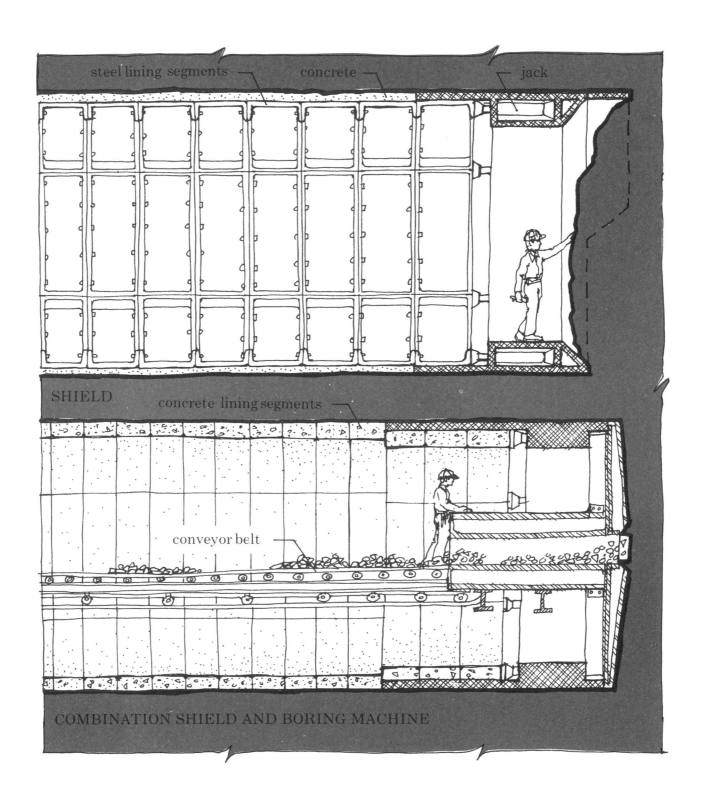

steel lining segments     concrete     jack

SHIELD     concrete lining segments

conveyor belt

COMBINATION SHIELD AND BORING MACHINE

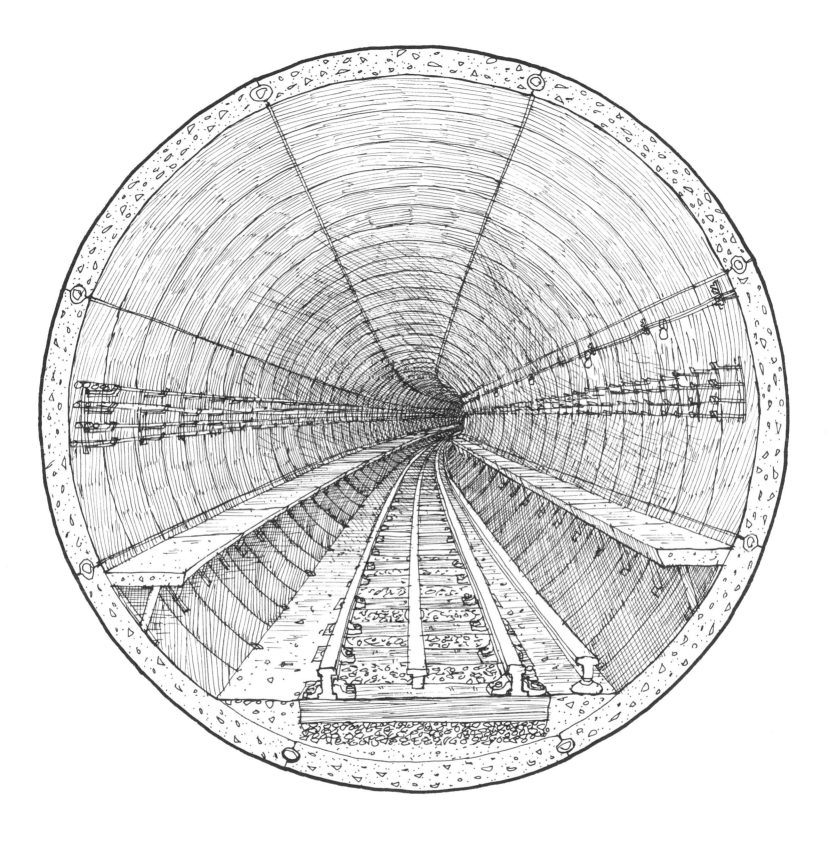

been moved. In either case the tunnel is permanently locked into the earth. A tunnel cut through solid rock doesn't need a shield and it is sometimes left unlined. To reduce the building time, excavation crews will work simultaneously from several different shafts.

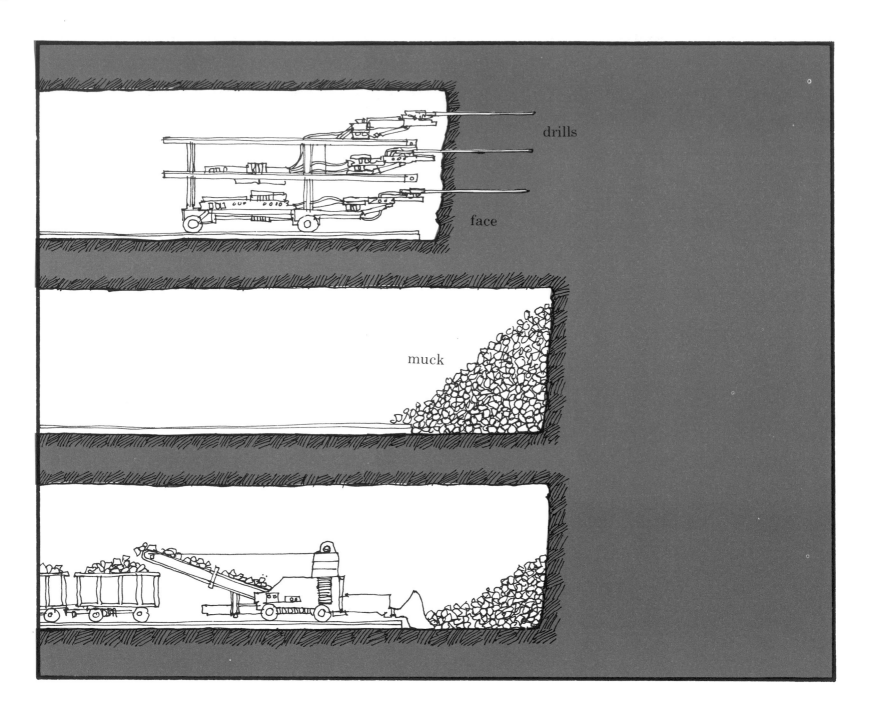

drills

face

muck

The face of a tunnel can be excavated in many ways. If necessary it can be dug by hand, but usually powerfull drills or a single large boring machine are used. When the tunnel is going through rock or very hard clay, the drill holes are filled with explosives, which, when ignited, reduce the face to rubble. As soon as the ventilation system has cleared the air, the muck is carried in small carts along a narrow track or along a conveyor belt to the nearest shaft.

When the material through which the tunnel is to be dug contains a lot of water, the pressure at the tunnel face must be increased to prevent that water from pouring in. First a thick concrete wall is built behind the shield to seal the tunnel. It is in the space between this wall and the face that the pressure will be increased. Then

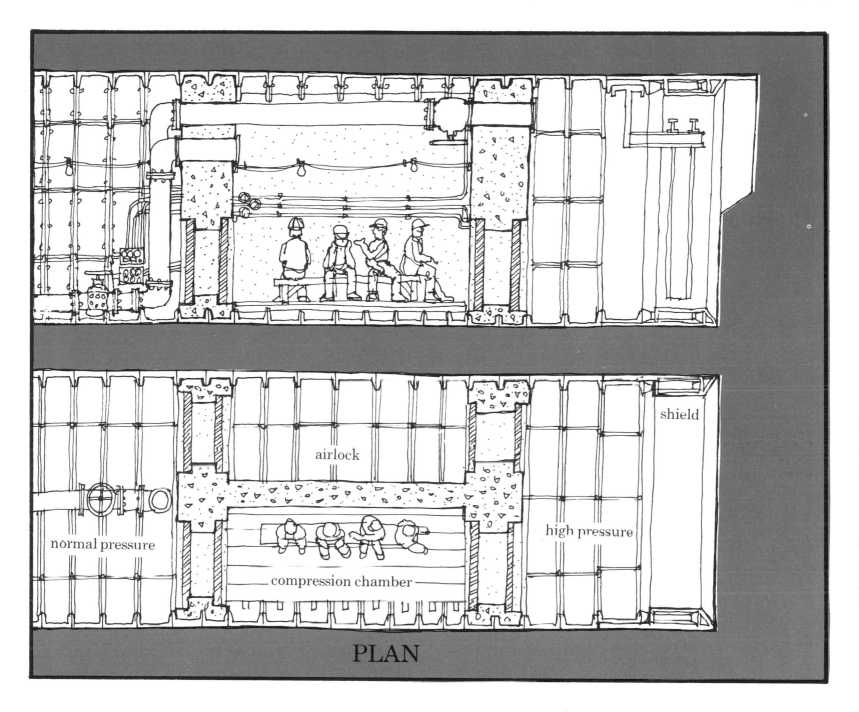

PLAN

a second concrete wall is built about ten feet behind the first, which also fits against the sides of the tunnel to create an airtight seal. The space between the walls is called a compression chamber and is entered through heavy steel doors located in both walls. Because of the difference between the pressure at the face and the pressure in the rest of the tunnel, workers traveling from one area to the other must spend a certain amount of time in the chamber. This way their bodies can adjust gradually as the pressure in the chamber is slowly changed to equal either the higher pressure at the face or the normal pressure towards the shaft. Special air locks built into the chamber enable equipment and muck to be passed through without breaking the seal between the two areas.

When a section of tunnel is complete the necessary structure for the tracks is constructed and the tracks themselves laid. Because the tunnel is cylindrical there is enough room between its side and that of the train so that the cables for power, signals, and lighting can be hung directly on the wall. Deep subway tunnels are usually made just large enough to hold one set of tracks, but when several tracks come together or a station is required the diameter is simply increased.

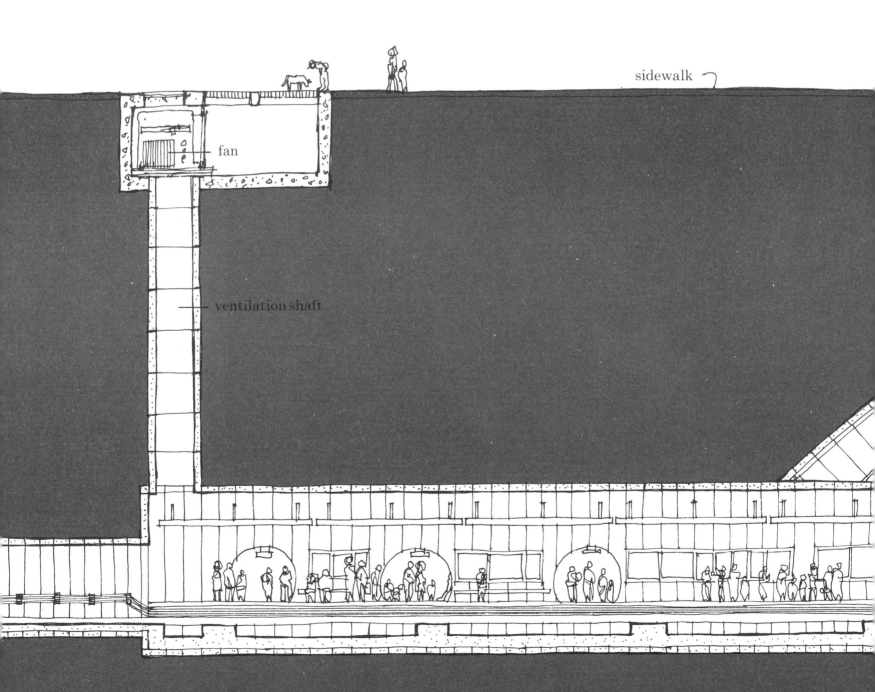

sidewalk

fan

ventilation shaft

While the train tunnels are being constructed, other tunnels and shafts are being excavated for elevators, escalators, and pedestrian crossover ramps between the different tracks. When the underground work is finished, many of the original construction shafts are used either for emergency stairways or for the large ventilating fans that force clean air throughout the system.

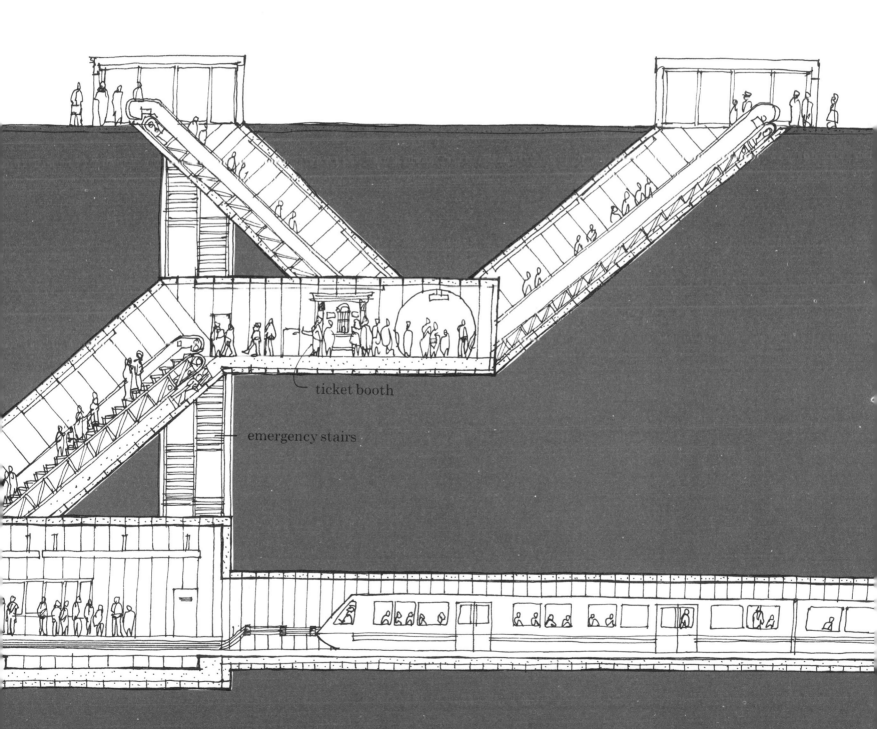

ticket booth

emergency stairs

With the completion of the subway, the last major artery through our intersection takes its place. Millions of tons of soil and rock have been removed to make way for the intricate network of structures and systems essential to life on the surface. Yet regardless of their importance, our awareness of the existence of this vast hidden complex depends almost entirely on a few seemingly insignificant clues. However, it is because of clues, such as an escaping column of steam, or the tip of a ladder rising above an open manhole, or the rumbling of trains below our feet, that we are reminded of the immense amount of technology on which we depend. And no matter how complex a picture our imaginations conjur up it could hardly be more amazing than the real underground.

# GLOSSARY

BEARING PILE  A shaft or column driven into the ground to act as a foundation by transferring the load that it supports through the bottom to the very firm soil or bedrock on which it rests.

BEDROCK  The solid crust of the earth, which often lies several hundred feet below the surface.

BELL  A cavity in the shape of a bell, which is scooped out at the base of a pier shaft to distribute the load over a greater area.

CAP  A concrete pad that ties the ends of piles together either in a cluster or row, which in turn supports a column or wall.

CATCH BASIN  A tank located under the street in which water is temporarily stored so that objects that might clog the storm drain system can settle to the bottom before the water enters the pipes.

CLUSTER  A closely spaced group of piles used to support the weight of a single column.

"CUT AND COVER"  The process of subway construction that involves digging the necessary cavity, constructing the tunnel in the cavity, and filling the cavity when the tunnel is complete.

DUCT  A protective pipe placed underground in which electrical and telephone cables are located.

DUCT BANK  Several rows of ducts grouped together and encased in concrete.

ENCLOSURE WALL  A concrete wall built around a site which extends from the basement to ground level yet does not serve as a foundation for the building above.

EXCAVATION  The digging out and removal of soil from a site.

FACE  The surface of the tunnel that is continually being dug away.

FILL  The material used to fill a trench after a pipe is laid or to rebuild the floor of an excavation to the required height.

FLOATING FOUNDATION  A continuous spread foundation that extends under an entire building replacing many separate footings.

FORMWORK  The temporary mold into which liquid concrete is poured to create a specific shape and any structure necessary to support that mold.

FOUNDATION  The structural system constructed below a building which transfers the weight of the building to the ground on which it stands.

FOUNDATION WALL  A wall (usually of concrete) built below ground level to transfer the weight of the exposed wall it supports to the footing on which it rests.

FRICTION PILE  A shaft or column that is hammered into the ground until the pressure or friction developed between the surface of the pile and the soil into which it is forced enables it to become a firm foundation on which to build.

FROST LINE  The level below the surface at which the soil is likely to freeze.

GATE KEY  A long-handled wrench that is used to open and close a valve.

GRADE  The angle or slope at which water and sewer pipes are laid to maintain a flow without pumping.

GRILLAGE  Rows of steel beams placed between the base of a steel column and the top of the concrete cap or pier on which it will rest to distribute the pressure over the surface more evenly.

INLET  An opening in the street surface, covered by a steel grate, through which water flows into a storm drain.

JACK  A machine that is capable of lifting a very heavy weight or of applying pressure to the two surfaces between which it is placed.

LAGGING  Vertical boards that are used to line a trench in order to prevent the soil from caving in.

MANHOLE  A room located underneath the street named after the hole in the surface of the street through which it is entered.

MUCK  The material removed during the process of boring a tunnel through the ground.

NEEDLE BEAMS  A type of underpinning in which horizontal steel beams are placed under a wall to temporarily carry the weight.

PIER  A column or shaft in the ground that serves as a foundation and is constructed by drilling a hole and filling it with concrete.

PIPE PILES  A type of underpinning in which steel tubes are driven into the ground below an existing wall to temporarily carry the weight.

RACKS  Metal brackets fastened to the walls of manholes and vaults on which electrical and telephone cables are hung.

REINFORCING  The steel rods or mesh embedded in concrete to strengthen it.

RETAINING WALL  A wall built around all or part of a site being excavated to prevent the sides from collapsing.

SEWER SYSTEM  The system through which all liquid waste from the city is carried to treatment plants.

SHAFTS  Vertical passages dug to the level of a proposed tunnel through which men, equipment, clean air, and muck are moved.

SHEETING  A retaining wall built of steel or wood or both.

SHEET PILES  Interlocking steel sheets driven into the ground around a site before excavation to act as a retaining wall.

SHIELD  A large steel tube in which the men work when boring deep tunnels through clay or unstable rock.

SHORES  Inclined wood or steel beams used to brace a retaining wall.

SITE  The term used to describe the exact location of a building that is to be constructed.

SOIL PROFILE  A vertical cross-section drawing of the ground showing the type and depth of each layer of material between the surface and bedrock.

SOLDIER BEAMS  Steel beams that are driven into the ground around a site before excavation and between which horizontal boards are slid to create a retaining wall as the soil is removed.

SPREAD FOUNDATION  A very common type of foundation that involves placing a flat concrete slab called a footing under each column or wall, thereby distributing the weight over a greater area.

STORM DRAINS  The pipe system built to carry away large amounts of water that sometimes accumulate quickly from storms or melting snow.

SUMP PIT  A small recess in the floor of a manhole into which any water in the manhole flows and from which it can be more easily pumped.

TRANSFORMER  The piece of equipment used for increasing and reducing the amount of electrical current passing through it.

UNDERPINNING  Temporary support placed under an existing building while its foundations are deepened or replaced.

UTILITIES  The more common life-supporting systems of a city and its inhabitants, including water supply, sewage removal, electricity, gas, steam, and telephone communication.

VALVE BOX  A vertical pipe located above each valve through which the valve is opened and closed.

VALVE  A metal gate installed in a pipe to shut off the flow of either water, steam, or gas.

VAULT  A room under the sidewalk in which transformers are located.

WATER TABLE  The distance below the surface at which the soil is completely saturated with water.

WELL POINTS  Pipes driven into the ground in and around a site through which water is drained in order to maintain a water table below the base of the excavation.

WINCH  A machine designed to wind up a cable or rope which is capable of pulling or lifting a heavy load.